SKIP
THE
CODE,
LOVE
THE
AI

This book and its content are a work of both the author and AI-generated content, showcasing the amazing collaborative potential of humans and AI. The information contained in this book, including questions and answers, is provided for informational purposes only. The author and publisher make no representations or warranties of any kind, express or implied, about the completeness, accuracy, reliability, suitability, or availability with respect to the book or the information, products, services, or related graphics contained the book for any purpose. Any reliance you place on such information is therefore strictly at your own risk. Always consult with qualified professionals for specific advice.

DEDICATED TO

Hanuman Ji

My father & mother

My brother

INTRODUCTION

I want to thank you and congratulate you for purchasing "Skip the Code, Love the AI"! My name is Uttam, and as a software engineer who's worked in MNCs and Fortune 500 companies, I've seen firsthand the incredible impact AI is having on businesses and individuals alike. I'm also aware of the growing interest in AI from people who don't have a coding background, and I'm excited to share my knowledge with you in a way that's accessible and engaging.

This book is for you if you've ever been curious about AI but felt intimidated by the technical jargon and the perceived need for coding skills. It's for those who've wondered if they could create art with a computer, build a robot, or simply understand how AI is changing the world around us, but thought it required a degree in rocket science.

Good news! You don't need to be a coding whiz to understand and appreciate AI. In fact, many of the most exciting applications of AI are designed to be accessible to everyone, regardless of their technical background. This book is your invitation to explore the magic of AI without the fear of getting lost in a sea of code.

Now, before any coders out there get their keyboards in a twist, let me clarify: Coding is a fantastic skill, and if you have the passion for it, go for it! This book is simply for those who might feel intimidated by the technical aspects and want a more accessible entry point into the world of AI.

In this book, we'll embark on a journey to demystify AI, uncover its secrets, and explore its real-world applications, all in a language that everyone can understand. We'll discover how AI is changing everything from customer service and healthcare to education and entertainment. And we'll learn how you can be a part of this exciting technological revolution, even if you "skip the code."

So, whether you're a student, a business professional, a creative artist, or simply a curious mind, get ready to fall in love with AI!

Contents

1
What is AI, really?

Artificial Intelligence, or AI, is like giving a computer the ability to think and act a bit like a human. At its core, AI is about creating systems that can tackle tasks that usually need human smarts, like recognizing a photo, understanding speech, or even guessing what movie you'd enjoy next. Think of it as a super-helpful assistant that doesn't just follow strict orders but learns from examples and gets better over time.

Imagine you're teaching a kid to spot dogs. You show them lots of dog pictures—big ones, small ones, fluffy ones—and say, "These are dogs." Soon, they can pick out a dog in a new photo. AI works the same way: you feed it data—like pictures, words, or numbers—and it finds patterns to make sense of things. For example, when you talk to a voice assistant on your phone, it's AI figuring out you said "play music," not "play moose," based on what it's heard before.

In a company, AI can do cool stuff like reading customer emails to spot complaints or predicting which products will sell best next month. It helps people focus on the big ideas while AI handles the repetitive bits—like sorting data or answering basic questions. For service-based jobs, like in tech support or consulting, AI might power a chatbot that keeps clients happy 24/7, freeing you up to solve trickier problems.

The magic isn't in the machine itself but in how it learns and adapts. It's why companies love it: AI can crunch numbers, spot trends, and even talk back. So, really, AI is just a tool that mimics a slice of human thinking, making life easier and work smarter!

2
How does AI make life easier with automation?

Automation with AI is like having a super-efficient teammate who never gets tired of the boring stuff. It's all about letting machines handle repetitive tasks. Think of it as handing over the grunt work—like sorting emails, filing paperwork, or tracking inventory—to a smart robot.

Here's how it works: AI doesn't just follow a script like an old-school computer program. It learns from what it sees and gets smarter over time. For example, imagine a company getting hundreds of customer emails daily. Without AI, someone's stuck reading them all, figuring out which ones need a quick reply or a deeper fix. With AI automation, the system can scan those emails, spot key words like "urgent" or "refund," and sort them into the right piles—or even send basic replies itself. That saves hours!

In a service-based job—like tech support for a client—AI can automate things like resetting passwords or checking system statuses. Instead of you typing the same answers over and over, an AI chatbot jumps in, freeing you to tackle bigger challenges, like designing a new solution for the client. This benefits everyone: customers receive prompt assistance, and employees can dedicate their expertise to more complex issues.

Businesses love this because it cuts time and costs. Picture a warehouse: AI can track stock levels, predict when to reorder, and even guide robots to pack boxes.

For HR folks, it might mean AI screening résumés to find top candidates faster, leaving the real decisions to you. At its heart, AI automation is like a tireless helper, streamlining the mundane so everyone—workers, companies, clients—can thrive.

3
What's an example of AI you use every day?

One AI you probably bump into daily is the voice assistant on your phone or smart speaker. When you say, "Hey [voice assistant], set a timer for 10 minutes," it's not just a fancy tape recorder—it's AI in action, quietly making your life smoother. How does it do that? It listens to your voice, figures out what you mean, and responds, all in a split second. That's something you use without even thinking about it!

Here's the breakdown: when you talk, the voice assistant's microphones catch the sound, and its AI—trained on millions of voice samples—turns your words into text. Then, another layer of AI digs into that text to understand your intent. Are you asking for a timer, the weather, or to play your favourite song? It's like a detective piecing together clues from how you speak—even if you mumble or have an accent. Once it gets it, it acts, setting that timer while you cook dinner or rush out the door.

For a service-based job—like working at a company that builds tech solutions—this is gold. Imagine a client asking, "How fast can your system answer questions?" You could point to voice assistants: it's AI that's quick, learns over time, and handles everyday tasks effortlessly. Beyond voice, AI is also in those movie recommendations you get, spotting patterns in what you watch to suggest a thriller over a rom-com, or in those navigation apps, predicting the fastest route based on traffic data it's crunched.

Why's this cool? It's AI doing the heavy lifting—listening, thinking, deciding—without you noticing. It's not some sci-fi robot; it's a tool baked into your routine, saving time and guesswork. Next time you ask your voice assistant for the news or a reminder, you're tapping into AI that's quietly become your daily sidekick!

4
How does AI learn to do its job?

AI learns to do its job a bit like a kid picking up a new skill—through examples, practice, and a little trial and error. Unlike a regular computer program with fixed rules, AI figures things out by studying data you give it. Imagine teaching a child to recognize apples. You'd show them red apples, green apples, even a slightly bruised one, and say, "These are apples." Over time, they spot the patterns—round shape, stem on top—and can pick an apple out of a fruit bowl. AI works the same way, just with way more examples and some clever math!

Here's how it goes: you feed AI a big pile of data—like photos, customer records, or voice clips—depending on what you want it to do. Say it's a chatbot for a service company. You'd give it tons of past chats: "Hi, I need help with my bill," or "Can you reset my password?" The AI analyses these, spotting common words and phrases, and learns what responses work best. It's not memorizing; it's finding the patterns—like noticing "bill" often means "send a statement."

The magic happens with something called a model—a kind of brain for the AI. Coders tweak this model using algorithms, which are like recipes for learning. The AI tests itself: "Did I get this right?" If it messes up—like thinking "bill" means "pill"—it adjusts, guided by feedback in the data. Over time, it gets sharper, predicting answers faster and more accurately.

For a job seeker in a service role, this matters because clients love AI that adapts—like a system that learns their preferences. HR might see it as a hiring tool, sifting résumés by learning what "good candidate" looks like. It's not instant; it takes data and tuning, but once trained, AI's like a pro who never forgets the playbook!

5
Why do companies love using AI?

Companies love AI because it's like hiring a superstar who works fast, spots things humans might miss, and saves a ton of money—all without needing a corner office! It's a game-changer for getting stuff done smarter and quicker. Picture a busy customer service team drowning in calls about "Where's my order?" AI steps in with a chatbot that answers instantly, 24/7, so the team can focus on trickier problems—like calming an upset client. That's one big reason: it handles the grind, letting people shine where creativity or empathy counts.

Another perk is AI's knack for finding gold in data. Say a company tracks sales—AI can dig through years of numbers and say, "Hey, your winter coats sell like crazy in November, stock up!" It's not guessing; it's spotting patterns humans might overlook, helping bosses make sharp decisions. For service-based firms—like IT support or consulting—this is huge. AI can predict when a client's system might crash, fixing it before they even notice, keeping everyone happy and contracts renewed.

Cost is a big draw too. Training AI might take effort, but once it's rolling, it's cheaper than hiring extra staff for repetitive tasks. Think data entry: instead of someone typing numbers all day, AI scans document, pulls the info, and plugs it into the system—done! HR loves this for recruiting—AI can skim hundreds of résumés, flagging the best fits, saving hours of manual work.

Plus, it's scalable. A small business might use AI to chat with a few customers; a big one scales it to millions. It's like a tool that grows with you. Companies adore AI because it's a tireless, brainy helper—boosting efficiency, cutting costs, and turning data into action. For job seekers, knowing this shows you get why businesses bet on AI—and how you can fit into that future!

6
What's the difference between a robot and AI?

Think of a robot and AI as a dynamic duo—like a body and a brain—that don't always come as a package deal. A robot is the physical part: a machine you can see and touch, like a vacuum cleaner rolling around your house or a mechanical arm stacking boxes in a warehouse. It's built to move, lift, or do something tangible, following instructions like a loyal worker. But without AI, it's just a dumb hunk of metal and gears, doing exactly what it's told—no thinking, no adapting.

AI, on the other hand, is the smarts—the software that can learn, decide, and figure things out. It doesn't need a body; it can live in your phone or a computer, like when a streaming service guesses you'll love a sci-fi flick based on your binge history. AI takes data—like voices, images, or numbers—and spots patterns to make choices. Pair it with a robot, though, and you've got magic! That vacuum cleaner? Add AI, and it's not just spinning in circles—it's mapping your floor, dodging your cat, and learning where the crumbs hide.

Here's a real example: in a service company, a robot might deliver mail around an office—cool, but basic if it just follows a taped line. Add AI, and it learns the fastest routes, avoids busy hallways, and even knows when to recharge. Meanwhile, AI alone might power a chatbot, helping clients without any physical form. The key difference? Robots do the muscle work; AI does the brain work.

For HR, this matters when hiring—do you need a coder for AI or an engineer for robots? For job seekers, it's a chance to shine: "I can tweak AI to make that delivery bot smarter!" Robots and AI can team up or stand solo, but together, they're unstoppable—turning clunky machines into clever helpers.

7
How can AI help a small business grow?

AI is like a secret weapon for small businesses—it's affordable, powerful, and levels the playing field against the big guys! For a small outfit—like a local bakery or a freelance consulting gig—AI can boost growth by saving time, wooing customers, and making smart moves without breaking the bank. It's not about fancy robots; it's about simple tools that pack a punch.

Take time-saving: a small business owner wears a dozen hats—baking, marketing, answering emails. AI can jump in with a chatbot, handling basic customer questions like "What time do you open?" or "Can you ship this?"—all day, every day. That frees the owner to focus on perfecting recipes or pitching to new clients. In a service-based role, like IT support, AI could scan client tickets, flagging urgent ones so you solve problems faster and look like a hero.

Then there's understanding customers. AI can dig into sales data— like which cupcakes fly off the shelf on Saturdays—and say, "Hey, bake more chocolate ones this weekend!" It's not guesswork; it's patterns from past buys, helping you stock what sells and skip what flops. For a consultant, AI might analyse client feedback, spotting trends like "they love quick responses," so you tweak your pitch to win more gigs.

Growth also comes from reaching people. AI can power cheap, targeted ads online—say, showing your bakery's ad to local dessert lovers on social media—without you hiring a marketing pro. Plus, it scales: as orders pile up, AI keeps handling chats or crunching numbers, no extra staff needed. For HR, it's a hiring perk—AI can screen applicants, finding folks who fit your vibe.

The best part? Tools like chatbots or data-crunchers are often plug-and-play now—no coding degree required. AI gives small businesses a brainy boost—more sales, happier customers, less stress—turning a little dream into a thriving reality!

8
What's one way AI is changing customer service?

One big way AI is shaking up customer service is through chatbots—those friendly little helpers you chat with online or over the phone. Imagine you're on a website, tracking a late package, and instead of waiting on hold for 20 minutes, a chat pops up: "Hi! I can check that for you—what's your order number?" That's AI in action, transforming how companies talk to customers by making it faster, easier, and available around the clock.

Here's how it works: a chatbot uses AI to understand what you type or say—thanks to something called Natural Language Processing, which is like teaching it to decode human chatter. Say you ask, "Where's my stuff?" It scans for keywords like "where" and "stuff," figures out you mean a delivery, and pulls the tracking info from a database—all in seconds. It's trained on tons of past conversations, so it knows "stuff" might mean "package" and can even handle typos or slang like "gimme an update."

For a service-based company—like one handling tech support for clients—this is a game-changer. Picture a flood of "My Wi-Fi's down!" messages. The chatbot jumps in, guiding folks through basic fixes—like rebooting the router—before a human steps in for trickier cases. It's not just speed; it's there 24/7, so a midnight glitch doesn't mean a cranky customer waiting till morning. Companies save on staffing, and customers feel heard without the muzak torture.

HR might love this for training—fewer reps needed for routine calls means more focus on hiring problem-solvers. Coders keep it running, tweaking the AI to catch new phrases. And for job seekers, it's a buzzword to drop: "I've seen how chatbots cut wait times!" It's not replacing humans—it's teaming up with them, making service snappier and letting real people shine where warmth or creativity counts most.

9
Can AI make mistakes—and why?

You bet AI can make mistakes—it's not some flawless sci-fi genius! Just like us, it trips up sometimes, and the reasons boil down to how it learns and what it's given to work with. Picture AI as a super-smart student: if you teach it with shaky lessons or throw curveballs it hasn't studied for, it's going to flub the test. Those slip-ups happen because AI isn't magic—it's a tool built on data, and that data can be its Achilles' heel.

Take a voice assistant, for example. You say, "Play jazz," but it hears "Play cats" and starts meowing tunes—if it plays anything at all! Why? Maybe it was trained on voices that don't sound like yours, or the room was noisy, and it guessed wrong. That's a biggie: bad or messy data. If AI learns from blurry photos, outdated records, or biased examples— like only hearing posh accents—it'll stumble when faced with real-world variety. In a service job, like analysing client feedback, AI might misread "great service" as negative if its training data skewed sarcastic.

Another reason is overthinking. Sometimes AI gets too cozy with its training data—like memorizing a cheat sheet instead of learning the subject. Then, when a new problem pops up, it's clueless. Think of a fraud detection AI: if it's only seen old scams, a fresh trick might slip by. Plus, it's not human—it can't "feel" context or double-check gut instincts like we do.

For HR, this means AI needs oversight; for coders, it's a challenge to clean data and tweak models. Job seekers can nod to it: "I know AI isn't perfect—I'd help spot its hiccups!" Mistakes don't mean AI's useless— they just show it's a partner, not a replacement, needing humans to guide it when the going gets weird.

10
How does AI in something like a voice assistant understand me?

When you talk to a voice assistant, it's like chatting with a clever detective who's piecing together your words—and it's all thanks to AI! It's not just hearing you; it's figuring out what you mean, step by step, in a way that feels almost human. Say you mumble, "Hey [voice assistant], turn on the lights." How does it get from your voice to flipping a switch? Let's unpack it.

First, the voice assistant's microphones catch your voice—every "um," slur, or background dog bark included. The AI kicks off with something called Automatic Speech Recognition, or ASR. It's like a translator that turns your spoken sounds into text, breaking down "turn on the lights" into words it can read. It's trained on millions of voices—accents, speeds, even kids shouting—so it's got a knack for guessing, even if you're not crystal clear.

Next comes the brainy part: Natural Language Understanding, or NLU. This is where the voice assistant decodes what you want. It spots "turn on" as a command and "lights" as the target, linking them to actions it knows—like controlling your smart bulbs. It's not just parroting; it's been fed tons of example phrases, so it can handle "switch the lights on" or "light up the room" too. Over time, it learns your quirks—like if you say "lamp" instead—or adjusts to your sloppy "lights."

For a service gig, like building client tools, this is gold: imagine coding a voice-activated system to answer "Check my account" for a bank. HR might see it as a productivity boost—fewer manual lookups. Job seekers can flex it: "I get how AI parses sloppy requests!" It's not perfect—yell "play jazz" in a storm, and it might flinch—but it's a tireless listener, refining itself with every chat to sound like it really gets you.

11
How does AI figure out what I'm typing in a search bar?

When you type something into a search bar—like "best pizza near me"—AI is quietly playing detective, figuring out what you really want, even if you're halfway through or misspelling "piza." It's not just waiting for you to hit enter; it's predicting, guessing, and refining as you go, making that search bar feel like it's reading your mind. How does it pull that off? It's a mix of clever tricks and a lot of behind-the-scenes learning.

First, AI uses something called autocomplete—or predictive text. It's been trained on gazillions of searches from people like you and me, spotting patterns in what we type. Start with "be" and it might suggest "best" because that's a common kick-off. Add "pi," and it's narrowing down to "pizza" based on what's popular or local. It's like a librarian who's seen every book request ever—she knows what you're likely after before you finish asking!

Then there's the smarts of understanding intent. AI doesn't just look at your letters; it guesses what's on your mind. Typing "pizza" in Mumbai? It assumes "near me" even if you skip it, pulling up local joints over some random Italian village. It's trained on location data, past searches, and even trends—like if everyone's hunting pizza on Friday nights. For a service job, think of coding a client's search tool: "Find my invoice" could trigger AI to fetch their latest bill, not someone else's.

It's not perfect—type "bat" and it might guess "Batman" over "battery"—but it learns. Every click you make teaches it what you meant, tweaking its guesses for next time. For HR, it's a productivity gem; for coders, it's algorithms at play. It's AI turning a few keystrokes into a mind-reading act—fast, friendly, and a little magical!

12
How AI can save time in an office?

One fantastic way AI saves time in an office is by automating scheduling—like a superhero assistant who juggles calendars without breaking a sweat! Picture a busy workplace: meetings to book, client calls to slot, team huddles to fit in. Normally, you're emailing back and forth—"Does 2 PM work?" "No, how about 3?"—wasting hours in a ping-pong of replies. AI swoops in with tools like smart scheduling assistants, cutting that chaos down to seconds.

Here's how it happens: an AI tool—like one built into your email software or a standalone app—scans everyone's calendars, spots free slots, and picks the best time for all. Say you're in HR setting up interviews for a new hire. You tell the AI, "Book five candidates next week," and it checks your team's availability, the candidates' preferences (if shared), and even time zone quirks if someone's remote—like a coder in Pune meeting a client in Delhi. Boom—it suggests "Tuesday, 11 AM," sends invites, and books the room, all while you sip your chai.

It's not just button-pushing; AI learns. It notices you hate early mornings or that the boss blocks Fridays, so it adapts, saving you from rescheduling headaches. For a service-based job—like consulting—it's a lifesaver: imagine coordinating a demo for a client across three cities. AI aligns it faster than you can type "Are you free?" Plus, it can nudge folks with reminders, slashing no-shows.

Why's this a big deal? Time's gold in an office—less faffing with schedules means more focus on real work, like cracking a project or prepping a pitch. HR sees happier teams; coders get uninterrupted coding sprints; job seekers can say, "I've seen AI streamline chaos!" It's not replacing you—it's clearing the clutter so you shine. That's AI: a quiet, tireless time-saver, making office life smoother one calendar slot at a time.

13
Can AI replace a human worker completely?

The big question—can AI kick humans out of their jobs entirely? Not quite! AI's a powerhouse, sure, but it's more like a trusty sidekick than a full-on replacement. It can take over tasks, mimic skills, and even outpace us in some areas, but there's a human spark it just can't replicate—yet. Let's dig into why it's not game over for workers, especially in an office or service gig.

AI shines at repetitive, predictable stuff. Think data entry: you used to type numbers into spreadsheets all day; now AI scans document and fills them in faster than you can blink. Or customer service—chatbots handle "Where's my order?" like champs, leaving no human drowned in basic queries. In a service-based role, like IT support, AI might troubleshoot a client's "printer won't print" before you pick up the phone. It's quick, tireless, and doesn't need a lunch break—pretty slick, right?

But here's the catch: AI struggles with the messy, human stuff. Imagine a client's furious about a late delivery—AI can apologize, but it can't feel their frustration or improvise a heartfelt fix like you can. Creativity's another wall—designing a campaign, brainstorming a pitch, or comforting a stressed teammate? AI can suggest, but it's you who brings the magic touch. Even in coding, AI writes chunks of code, but a human coder decides what's clever or clunky.

For HR, this is key: AI might screen résumés, but you judge the vibe in an interview. Job seekers can lean into this—"I bring the empathy AI can't!" Truth is, AI's a partner, not a usurper. It clears the grunt work— like scheduling or sorting—so you focus on what machines can't: connecting, inventing, feeling. Completely replacing humans? Nuh, we're too messy, too brilliant. AI's here to lift us up, not shove us out— think teammate, not terminator!

14
Why do some people call AI a 'black box'?

Ever heard AI called a "black box" and wondered what's up with that? It's a nickname that pops up because, for all its brilliance, AI can be a bit of a mystery—even to the folks who build it! Imagine a magician pulling a rabbit from a hat: you see the trick, but how it happens? No clue. AI's like that—spitting out answers or decisions, but the "how" inside stays hidden, murky, like peering into a sealed-up box.

Here's why: most modern AI, especially the brainy stuff like neural networks, learns by crunching massive piles of data—think millions of pictures or chats. It tweaks itself, layer by layer, spotting patterns we can't easily trace. Say you ask it, "Is this email spam?" It says "yes," but if you ask, "Why?"—good luck getting a straight answer! It's not like a recipe with clear steps; it's more like a chef who just knows the dish tastes right. For a service job, like analysing client data, AI might predict who'll buy, but explaining "why this guy?" gets fuzzy.

That opacity spooks people. HR might worry: "If AI picks candidates, how do I know it's fair?" Coders tweak it, but even they can't always unpack every twist—too many gears turning inside. In India, where trust matters—like choosing a vendor for a project—a "black box" AI suggesting "Go with them" without reasoning can feel off. Some call it a trust issue: if you can't see the logic, how do you rely on it?

It's not all AI—just the fancy, deep-learning kind. Simpler AI might show its math, but the cutting-edge stuff? Mysterious. Job seekers can nod to this: "I'd ensure AI's choices make sense to clients!" It's a black box because the brilliance is locked inside—amazing, but a puzzle we're still cracking.

15
What's the simplest task AI can do for a company?

When you think AI, you might picture robots running the show, but the simplest task it can do for a company is something as basic as sorting emails—like a digital clerk with lightning speed! It's not flashy, but it's a quiet hero in any office, especially for service-based firms juggling client messages or HR teams buried in inbox chaos. Anyone can grasp this—it's AI at its most down-to-earth.

Here's the deal: companies get flooded with emails daily—queries, complaints, spam, you name it. Without AI, someone's stuck sifting through, deciding what's urgent or junk. Enter AI: you set it up with a few rules or examples—like "flag anything with 'urgent'" or "bin 'win a free trip'"—and it learns to sort them into folders faster than you can say "coffee break." It's not reinventing the wheel; it's just scanning words, matching patterns, and plopping emails where they belong. Many email providers now use AI to automatically sort emails into categories like 'Primary,' 'Social,' and 'Promotions.'

For a service gig—like IT support—it might tag "server down" emails as priority, so you jump on the big fires first. HR could use it to spot job applications in a sea of "Re: Meeting" threads, saving hours of scrolling. It's simple because it doesn't need fancy tech—just some training data (past emails) and a basic algorithm to spot "important" versus "ignore." Even a small startup could use AI tools to automate email sorting and see immediate benefits.

Why's it great? Time saved, stress slashed, and no genius coder required—off-the-shelf AI can handle it. Job seekers can say, "I'd streamline workflows with this!" It's not curing cancer—it's mundane magic, proving AI's less about sci-fi and more about making every day work a breeze. That's the simplest trick in its book, and it's a winner!

16
How does AI know what ads to show me online?

Ever wonder why you scroll through a social media app and see ads for shoes you browsed last week? That's AI playing matchmaker between you and the internet's ad world! It's not psychic—it's just really good at piecing together clues about you, like a nosy friend who knows your wishlist. For companies, it's a goldmine; for you, it's why that biryani deal pops up right when you're hungry.

Here's how it works: AI tracks what you do online—nothing creepy, just patterns. Clicked on a saree while online shopping? Watched a travel vlog? It's watching. Cookies—little digital breadcrumbs—follow you across sites, feeding AI data like "likes fashion" or "plans a Goa trip." Add in your location (Mumbai? Rural UP?), past buys, even what you've searched for, and it builds a mini-profile. Ever searched "best laptop" during a sale? Suddenly, laptop ads are everywhere—AI's connecting the dots.

Then it gets clever. Using algorithms—fancy math recipes—it predicts what you'll bite on. It's trained on millions of people: "Folks who buy kurtas often grab jewelry next." So, if you're eyeing a kurta, bam—earring ads! It's not random; it's a guess based on what's worked before. For a coder, this is machine learning at play—tweaking itself with every click. HR might see it as targeting talent—ads for courses if you're job-hunting.

This targeted advertising is widely used. It's not perfect—buy a gift once, and AI might hound you with baby gear for months—but it learns. Click "not interested," and it adjusts. Job seekers can flex this: "I get how AI targets clients!" It's AI turning your digital footprints into a billboard just for you—smart, sneaky, and oh-so-effective.

17
What's the difference between AI and just a regular computer program?

Think of a regular computer program as a cook following a strict recipe—step-by-step, no surprises. Now picture AI as a chef who invents dishes by tasting and tweaking as they go. That's the big difference: a regular program does exactly what you tell it, while AI learns, adapts, and sometimes even surprises you! It's a shift from rigid rules to something more alive, and that's why companies—and jobs—are buzzing about it.

A regular program is like a calculator: punch in "2 + 2," and it spits out "4" because you coded it that way. It's predictable—great for payroll software spitting out salaries or a game moving Pac-Man left when you hit the arrow. But it's dumb as a brick if you throw it a curveball—like asking it to guess your next move. No learning, no thinking, just "do this, then that."

AI, though? It's got a brain—or at least pretends to!

Feed it data—like customer chats from a service desk—and it figures out patterns without you spelling it out. [1] "Lots of 'urgent' emails get quick replies," it notices, then starts flagging them itself. It's trained, not just programmed. Take a voice assistant, for example: say "play music," and it learns you mean Bollywood over time—no hardcoded "if this, then that" list, just a system that evolves.

For HR, it's why AI screens résumés better than a static filter—it spots "good fit" beyond keywords. Coders love it because it's less babysitting—teach it once, and it grows. Job seekers can say, "I know AI bends where programs break!" The catch? Regular programs are simpler, cheaper for basic tasks; AI's heftier, needing data and tuning. But that flexibility—learning from a messy world? That's AI's edge over the old-school code cookbook.

18
How can AI help with hiring new people?

Hiring's a slog—piles of resumes, endless interviews, and that gut-wrenching "Did we pick the right one?" AI swoops in like a smart assistant, making it faster, sharper, and less of a headache, especially for HR folks in busy service firms. It's not about replacing the human touch but supercharging it—think of it as a sieve that filters gold from gravel so you can focus on the gems.

First, AI tackles the resume avalanche. Instead of you squinting at 200 PDFs, it scans them in seconds, spotting keywords like "Python" or "customer service" that match the job. But it's not just a word-finder—it learns what "good" looks like from past hires. Did top performers have "team player" or "3 years' experience"? AI flags similar profiles, cutting your shortlist from chaos to a tidy dozen. With the abundance of online job applications, AI is a lifesaver for sifting talent fast.

Then there's screening. AI chatbots can ping candidates with quick questions—"Tell me about a project"—and gauge answers for buzzwords or even tone, weeding out mismatches before you waste a call. Some tools even analyse video interviews, catching smiles or confidence in voice—stuff you'd notice but faster. For a service gig, like IT support, it might test "Can you troubleshoot?" without you typing a quiz.

It's not flawless—AI might miss a diamond in the rough if their resume skips jargon—but it's a start. Coders build these tools, tweaking them to spot skills like "AWS" for a client. Job seekers can prep for it: "I'll shine past the bots!" For HR, it's time saved—less grunt work, more strategy, like picking culture fits in final rounds. AI's your hiring wingman, crunching data so you make the call with clearer eyes—hiring smarter, not harder.

19
What's one thing AI can't do that humans can?

AI's a wizard at crunching numbers and spotting patterns, but one thing it can't touch is feeling genuine empathy—the kind humans dish out without a manual. Think about a friend consoling you after a rough day: they don't just say "Sorry," they get it, share a laugh, maybe even cry with you. That's a human superpower—understanding emotions in a raw, messy, real way—and AI's still stuck on the sidelines, faking it at best.

Picture this: you're in a service job, like a call centre, and a customer's raging about a late delivery—tears, shouting, the works. AI can churn out a polite "We apologize for the delay" based on scripts it's learned, but it doesn't feel the sting of their frustration. It can't pick up that quiver in their voice and think, "This person needs a human touch," then pivot to a joke or a heartfelt promise to fix it. Humans do that instinctively—reading the room, bending rules, offering a comforting presence even over the phone. AI? It's a robot with a rulebook, not a heart.

Why's this a gap? AI runs on data—past chats, word patterns—but emotions aren't tidy numbers. It might mimic empathy, like a chatbot saying "I'm here for you," but it's a guess, not a connection. Coders can tweak it to sound warmer, but they can't code a soul. HR knows this—AI might rank candidates, but it's you sensing who'll gel with the team. Job seekers can lean in: "I bring the warmth AI misses!"

In many situations, where relationships and emotional connection are crucial—think negotiating a deal or supporting a teammate—empathy is king. AI can crunch sales or fix bugs, but it won't offer a hug or share a gut feeling. That's us—messy, feeling humans—holding a card AI can't play, no matter how smart it gets.

20
Why does AI need so much data to work?

AI's like a kid learning to ride a bike—it needs tons of practice runs to stop wobbling, and for AI, that practice is data! Without a mountain of examples—pictures, words, numbers—it's clueless, like trying to guess a recipe without tasting food. Data's the fuel that powers its smarts, teaching it what to do, how to spot patterns, and when to tweak its guesses. The more it gets, the better it rides.

Think of it this way: if you want AI to recognize cats, you can't just show it one fluffy tabby and call it a day. It needs thousands—big cats, small cats, grumpy cats—to figure out "cat" means fur, whiskers, and a tail, not just "that one photo." Same goes for a service job, like predicting client churn. Feed it years of customer records—calls, buys, complaints—and it learns "these folks who cancel whine about delays." Skimp on data, and it's blind, guessing wildly.

Why so much? AI doesn't think like us—it's not born with common sense. We see a dog and know it barks; AI needs hundreds of barks to connect the dots. It's all about patterns: the more examples, the clearer the picture. Coders call this training—piling data into algorithms till the AI "gets it." Think of training a chatbot for a customer support helpline—tons of "Where's my order?" chats teach it to nail the reply, not fumble.

HR might wonder: "Why not less?" Well, little data risks mistakes—like AI thinking only people in one city order pizza because that's all it saw. More data means broader smarts, fewer flops. Job seekers can flex this: "I'd ensure AI's fed right!" It's not greedy—it's just how AI builds its brain, one data crumb at a time, turning raw info into real-world wins.

21
How does a smart speaker wake up when I call it?

Ever shouted your smart speaker's wake word across the room and watched it light up, ready to roll? It's not just sitting there eavesdropping—it's AI doing a neat little dance to catch its name and spring into action. That wake-up trick is a blend of always-on listening and clever tech, making your smart speaker feel like a buddy who's always got an ear out for you.

Here's the magic: the smart speaker's microphones are live 24/7, sipping every sound—your TV, the dog barking, your off-key singing. But it's not recording everything—that'd be a privacy mess! Instead, it's running a tiny AI brain locally, right in the device, listening for one thing: its "wake word." This is a pattern it's trained to spot, kind of like how you perk up hearing your name in a crowd. It's got a library of wake word sounds—different accents, pitches, even a sleepy mumble—built from millions of voices so it won't miss yours.

When it hears a match—say, your cheerful "Hey [device name], play Bollywood!"—the AI flips a switch. That's the signal to wake up, start recording your full command, and send it to the cloud for the big brains to decode. Before that, it's just humming along, tossing out random noise like "blah blah" without saving a peep. Coders fine-tune this wake-word detector to avoid false alarms—like similar-sounding words—so it's not jumping at shadows.

For a service gig, think of tweaking this for a client's "Hey, Support!" hotline—same idea, custom trigger. HR might see it as effortless tech; job seekers can say, "I get how AI listens smart!" Even in noisy environments, it's a champ at filtering chaos to catch your call. It's not spooky—it's just AI, ears on, waiting for its cue to shine!

22
What's an example of AI making a boring job fun?

Imagine a job that's a total yawn—like counting inventory in a dusty warehouse, ticking off boxes of soap or rice bags all day. Yikes, right? Now toss in AI, and it's like turning a chore into a game! One killer example is how AI powers smart scanners—think handheld gadgets or even drones—that zip around, tallying stock, leaving you to play captain instead of pencil-pusher. It's a dull task flipped into something almost cool.

Here's how it works: instead of scribbling numbers on a clipboard, you've got an AI scanner that "sees" barcodes or labels with cameras and brains baked in. Point it at a shelf—or let a drone buzz overhead—and it counts everything, fast as lightning. It's trained on heaps of images, so it knows a shampoo bottle from a cereal box, even if they're jumbled. Your job? Steer the tech, check its work, and fix the odd hiccup—like when it mistakes a shadow for a stack. Suddenly, you're not a counter—you're a tech-savvy troubleshooter!

Picture a small retail store gone digital—AI tallies stock while the owner chats up customers, not hunched over a ledger. It's fun because it's interactive: you're guiding a gadget, watching it nail (or flub) the count, maybe even racing it for kicks. For coders, it's a playground—tweaking AI to spot a product in dim light. HR sees happier workers; no one's dozing off mid-shift. Job seekers can flex: "I'd turn stock checks into a breeze!"

It's not just speed—AI adds a dash of play. You're not buried in monotony; you're teaming with a bot, cracking a puzzle. Sure, it's still work, but it's less "ugh" and more "let's see what this thing can do!"—a boring gig reborn as a mini-adventure.

23
How can AI spot a mistake in a report?

AI spotting a mistake in a report is like having a super-sharp proofreader who never sleeps—it catches slip-ups humans might miss, fast and fuss-free! Imagine a sales report: numbers, dates, names, all jumbled across pages. A typo—like "1000" instead of "100"—could mess up budgets or deals. AI dives in, sniffing out errors by learning what "right" looks like and flagging what's off, saving you from spreadsheet nightmares.

Here's the trick: AI's trained on heaps of reports—past ones that worked and ones with blunders. It learns patterns—like sales totals usually match item counts, or dates don't jump to 2030 overnight. Say you're in a service gig, like managing client invoices. You feed AI a stack of old invoices—some with fat-fingered totals or misspelled city names. It builds a map of normal: totals add up, cities spell right. Then, it scans your new report. "Wait, this profit's 10 times last month's—fishy!" It flags it, maybe even highlights the rogue cell.

It's not just math—AI can catch funky text too. Think of a number format error—it knows that's a glitch from how numbers are typically displayed. AI can adapt to different language conventions and formats if trained right, spotting inconsistencies and errors. Coders tweak it to learn company lingo; HR loves it for clean payrolls—no one gets overpaid. Job seekers can say, "I'd use AI to keep reports tight!"

It's not foolproof—feed it messy training data, and it might miss the mark—but it's a hawk-eyed helper. It cross-checks, compares, and pings you: "This looks wonky, boss." You fix it, not hunt it. AI turns error-spotting from a slog into a quick ping—less stress, more trust in the numbers.

24
Why do companies use AI to talk to customers?

Companies lean on AI to chat with customers because it's like having a tireless, quick-on-the-draw assistant who keeps everyone happy without burning out! It's not just a tech flex—it's about speed, scale, and saving a buck, all while keeping that "we're here for you" vibe. In a world where customers expect answers now—not tomorrow—AI's the ace up their sleeve.

Take a busy e-commerce site during a big sale. Thousands of folks asking, "Where's my order?" or "Can I return this item?" Without AI, you'd need an army of reps, and even then, wait times would crawl. Enter AI chatbots: they jump in, trained on heaps of past chats to reply—"Your package is in transit, ETA tomorrow!"—in seconds. It's 24/7, no coffee breaks, handling hundreds at once. AI keeps the flood of inquiries from drowning the support team.

Why else? It's cheap—sort of. Training AI costs upfront, but once it's rolling, it's less than hiring extra staff for rote stuff like "Check my balance." Plus, it learns—mess up "When's delivery?" once, and it tweaks to nail it next time, unlike a script-reading human who might not care. For service gigs, like telecom support, it's a lifesaver: AI handles "Why's my net slow?" so reps tackle thornier fixes.

HR sees less burnout; coders build the bots, making them chatty and helpful. Customers don't always love it—AI can't always handle complex or emotionally charged situations—but it frees humans for that. Job seekers can nod: "I'd pair AI with my people skills!" Companies use it because it's fast, scalable, and lets them say "We've got you" without breaking the bank—keeping wallets and wait times slim.

25
What's the first step to start using AI in a business?

Diving into AI for a business feels big, but the first step is simple: figure out what problem you want it to solve—like picking a target before you swing! It's not about splashing cash on fancy tech right away; it's about knowing where AI can make your life easier, whether you're a small shop or a buzzing service firm. Get this right, and the rest falls into place.

Start by looking at your daily grind. Got a pile of customer emails clogging your inbox? Maybe AI can sort them. Losing hours scheduling client calls? AI could match calendars in a snap. For HR, it might be sifting résumés; for a coder, automating code tests; for a service gig, like a travel agency, predicting hot destinations. Think of a small store wanting to track what sells—AI could spot trends and help optimize inventory. The trick is pinning down a pain point—something repetitive, data-heavy, or just plain tedious.

Why this first? AI's not a magic wand—it needs a job to do. Without a clear "Solve this," you're tossing money at a shiny toy that sits unused. Take a break with your team: "What sucks up our time?" Jot down ideas—maybe it's chasing late payments or guessing stock needs. Pick one that's doable, not "fix world hunger." A consultancy might start small: "Let's use AI to flag urgent client queries."

Then you're ready for step two—data and tools—but that's later. Coders can say, "I'd code it to fit!" HR can plan training around it. Job seekers shine: "I'd spot where AI helps!" It's not tech-first; it's problem-first—grounded, practical, like plotting a road trip before you fuel up. Nail this, and AI's your ally, not a buzzword.

26
How does AI decide what's important in a pile of data?

Imagine dumping a messy pile of data—like customer emails, sales stats, or call logs—on AI's desk and saying, "Find what matters!" AI doesn't shrug—it digs in like a detective, sifting through the chaos to spotlight what's key. But how? It's not random—it's trained to weigh clues, spot patterns, and zero in on what moves the needle, whether for a service firm or an HR dashboard.

Here's the gist: AI starts with a goal—like "boost sales" or "flag complaints." You feed it heaps of data, say, past orders from a retailer: dates, items, prices. It's taught what's "important" by examples—maybe high sales days or big refunds. Using algorithms—think fancy sorting recipes—it ranks stuff based on impact. A trick called "feature importance" helps: it might see "weekend purchases" spike profits more than "weekday colours picked," so it flags weekends as the star.

Take a real case: a telecom service wants to cut churn. AI gets call logs, billing gripes, data usage. It learns—maybe from coders tweaking it—that "dropped calls" predict cancellations way more than "plan cost." It's not guessing; it's math—stats like correlation or weights in a model nudge it to prioritize. It might notice that service outages are a stronger predictor of churn than pricing changes—context it picks up from the pile.

HR might use this to find top talent traits—AI could say "team projects" beat "GPA" in past hires. Job seekers can flex: "I'd guide AI to focus!" It's not flawless—bad data can skew it, like mistaking noise for signal—but coders tune it, cutting fluff. AI decides by learning what's tied to your goal, then shining a light on it—turning a data mess into a tidy "Here's what counts!"

27
What's one way AI can predict if a customer will leave?

One slick way AI predicts if a customer's about to bolt is by sniffing out warning signs in their behaviour—like a fortune-teller reading tea leaves, but with data! It's called churn prediction, and companies, especially service-based ones like telecoms or streaming apps, love it. AI spots the "I'm outta here" vibe before you lose that subscription or client, giving you a heads-up to win them back.

Here's how it works: AI digs into past customer records—think call logs, billing history, or app usage. It's fed data on folks who've left: maybe they called support five times in a month, drastically reduced their usage, or grumbled online. AI learns these red flags by comparing leavers to stayers, building a pattern—like "lots of complaints plus low usage equals trouble." Then it scans current customers, flagging ones who fit the mold.

Take an example: Priya's been with a streaming service but hasn't watched in weeks and skipped her last payment reminder. AI notices— she's mirroring folks who cancelled before. It's not just guesswork; it uses math—like probabilities or decision trees—to weigh clues. "Late payments? 20% risk. No logins? 50%!" It might catch a combination of factors like reduced usage and account inactivity as a strong indicator of potential churn.

For coders, this is tweaking models to spot "churn signals" like a sudden drop-in activity. HR might use it to keep staff—same idea, different data. Job seekers can say, "I'd use AI to save clients!" It's not perfect—Priya might just be busy—but it's a crystal ball with stats, not magic. Companies jump on this to offer deals—like "Free month, Priya!"—before she's gone. AI's your early warning system, turning "See ya!" into "Stay a bit longer?"

28
How can AI automate checking someone's job application?

AI can take the grind out of checking job applications by acting like a super-speedy HR assistant—scanning résumés, asking questions, and flagging the best fits without you lifting a finger! It's a game-changer for service firms or any company swamped with applicants, cutting hours of manual sifting into minutes while keeping things sharp and fair—mostly.

Here's the play: AI starts with the résumé pile. Say an IT firm gets 500 applications for a coder gig. You feed it past hires' profiles—folks who nailed it with "Python, 3 years, teamwork." AI learns what clicks, then scans new PDFs or online forms, hunting keywords like "Java" or "client projects." It's not just word-matching—it ranks candidates by how close they fit, maybe scoring "4 years Python" higher than "1 year." Tools like these even pull data from LinkedIn, filling gaps.

Next, it can chat! AI bots ping applicants—"Tell me about a challenge you solved"—and read replies. Trained on tons of answers, it spots red flags (vague ramblings) or gold stars ("Fixed a client bug in 2 days"). It might ask, "Ever handled a high-pressure project with tight deadlines?"—adapting to the specific needs and context of the job. Some even analyse video intros, gauging confidence or clarity, though that's trickier.

For HR, it's a time-saver—shortlist done before lunch. Coders tweak it to weigh skills like "AWS" for a client's needs. Job seekers prep for it: "I'd ace the bot's quiz!" It's not perfect—AI might miss a gem with a funky résumé or bias toward buzzwords—but it's tenable. You set the rules; it runs the race, flagging "Interview these 10!" It's automation with brains—less slog, more focus on the human bit: picking who vibes with the team.

29
What's the difference between supervised and unsupervised learning?

Supervised and unsupervised learning are like two ways of teaching AI—one's a hands-on coach, the other's a "figure it out" vibe. They're the backbone of how AI learns, and knowing the difference can make you sound savvy, whether you're in HR, coding, or chasing a service gig. It's all about how much guidance AI gets—or doesn't—to tackle data.

Supervised learning is the teacherly one. You give AI a stack of data with answers attached—like showing it pics labelled "cat" or "dog." It's trained to spot patterns: "Whiskers? Cat!" You're holding its hand, feeding it examples—say, past sales tagged "hit" or "flop"—so it predicts the next big seller. Think of a busy call centre using old chats to teach AI: "Complaint = urgent." It's got a clear goal—match the dots—and coders test it: "Did it guess right?" It's great for specific tasks, like HR spotting top hires from labelled résumés.

Unsupervised learning? No hand-holding here! You dump a messy pile—like customer purchases, no labels—and say, "Find something useful." AI digs in, grouping stuff by patterns it discovers: "These folks buy rice and dal together." It's a bit wild—think clustering shoppers into groups based on their purchase history without predefining those groups. No right answers, just insights—like a service firm finding hidden client types to target. It's trickier to steer but shines when you don't know what's in the data.

The catch? Supervised needs tons of prepped data—time-heavy. Unsupervised's freer but vaguer—coders tweak it to avoid nonsense groups. Job seekers can flex: "I'd use supervised to predict, unsupervised to explore!" It's like strict parenting versus letting AI roam—both build smarts, just differently, and companies mix them to win.

30
How does AI help a company save money on energy bills?

AI can slash a company's energy bills by acting like a super-smart power manager—watching, tweaking, and predicting usage so the meter doesn't spin out of control! For a service firm—like an IT hub or call centre—it's a quiet money-saver, cutting costs without dimming the lights or sweating the staff. It's all about spotting waste and nailing efficiency, one watt at a time.

Picture a busy office, buzzing with ACs, computers, and coffee machines. AI steps in with sensors tracking power—when lights blaze in empty rooms or ACs blast at midnight. It's trained on past usage: "Friday afternoons dip low—half the team's WFH." So, it dims lights or tweaks thermostats automatically, not just on a timer like old tech, but smartly—learning patterns. Maybe it notices "humidity spikes AC use" and pre-cools smarter, not harder.

It goes deeper with prediction. Feed AI data—weather forecasts, staff schedules, even client call peaks—and it guesses: "Tomorrow's quiet, cut power 20%." It might prioritize—keep servers humming, skip the breakroom fridge. Big factories use this too—AI spots a machine guzzling juice and flags it for a fix before bills balloon.

For coders, it's building models to crunch sensor data; HR sees happier budgets, not frozen offices. Job seekers can say, "I'd trim costs with AI!" It's not cheap upfront—sensors and setup sting—but savings pile up fast. A startup might save significantly each year. It's not perfect—bad data might misjudge—but it's a hawk on waste, turning "lights on, nobody home" into "power down, profits up." AI's your energy whisperer—green vibes, fatter wallet!

31
Why might an AI chatbot misunderstand what I say?

An AI chatbot can trip over your words like a distracted friend—smart, but not always on the ball! It's built to chat like a human, but misunderstandings sneak in because it's juggling tech limits, messy human quirks, and the wild soup of language. Whether you're asking a service bot "Where's my refund?" or testing a voice assistant, here's why it might miss the mark.

One big hiccup? It's all about the data it's trained on. If you say, "Gimme my cash back" with a strong accent or using slang, but it's learned from different speech patterns, it might misinterpret your words. It's pattern-matching—sound to words—but if your slang, tone, or unique way of speaking wasn't in the mix, it flounders. Coders feed it voice samples, but the diversity of languages and accents can sometimes outpace the training.

Context's another trap. Say "Book it" to a travel bot. Ticket or hotel? It guesses from past chats, but if you meant "Cancel it" last time, it's lost. It's not thinking—it's mimicking, piecing your words against a script. Background noise can also muddy the waters; it might misinterpret your request due to loud sounds. Noisy data, no win.

Then there's the tech itself. It breaks your speech into bits—sound, then text, then meaning. A glitch at any step—like choppy audio or a weak "intent" model—means "Pay now" becomes "Play now." HR might see cranky clients; job seekers can say, "I'd tune it for clarity!" It's not dumb—just limited by what it's heard and how it's built. More chats, better data—including diverse accents and speech patterns—fix it over time. Till then, it's a keen listener with occasional earwax!

32
What's a common problem when training AI with data?

Training AI with data sounds straightforward—feed it info, let it learn—but a sneaky problem keeps popping up: bad data! It's like teaching a kid with a dodgy textbook; if the lessons are off, the AI picks up nonsense instead of smarts. This "garbage in, garbage out" snag trips up even the slickest systems, whether for service firms or HR dashboards, and it's a headache coders know all too well.

Here's the rub: AI needs heaps of data—like customer calls or sales logs—to spot patterns. But if that data's messy, incomplete, or biased, it's toast. Say you're training a chatbot for a bank. You give it old chats, but half are missing replies, some have misspellings or incorrect information, and most are from one type of customer, not representing the full diversity of your client base. AI learns wonky—it might misinterpret words, ignore certain accents or dialects, and fail to understand the nuances of customer requests. That's bad data: gaps, errors, or a skewed slice of reality.

Why's it common? Real-world data's a mess—humans typo, skip fields, or log weird stuff like "N/A" for age. Think of handwritten forms scanned wrong or notes with mixed languages that AI can't parse. Bias creeps in too—if your training data only represents a narrow slice of your customer base, it will struggle to understand and serve the rest. Coders fight this, cleaning data—fixing typos, filling blanks—but it's a slog. Miss it, and AI overfits—memorizing quirks like "all complaints are Tuesday"—or underperforms, missing the big picture.

HR might see AI flag wrong hires; job seekers can say, "I'd scrub data right!" It's not AI's fault—it's a mirror of what you give it. Fix it with diverse, tidy data—representing the full spectrum of your customers or users—and it sings. Till then, bad data's the gremlin, turning "smart" into "sorry, what?"

33
How can AI make a supply chain run smoother?

AI can turn a clunky supply chain into a slick, flowing dance—like a traffic cop clearing jams before they snarl! For service firms—like logistics or retail—it's a backstage hero, keeping goods moving from warehouse to doorstep with fewer hiccups. It's all about seeing ahead, tweaking on the fly, and dodging delays.

Take a real case: a company shipping phones across a large country. Normally, it's chaos—trucks late, stock piling up, or one region running dry while another's overstocked. AI jumps in with data—past deliveries, weather, holiday spikes—and predicts: "Big holiday season coming, double phones to this major area." It's trained on years of "what happened when," spotting that heavy rain slows trucks or certain events boost orders in specific regions. It's not guessing—it's crunching patterns to say, "Send now, not next week."

Then it optimizes. AI maps routes—suggesting alternate paths to avoid traffic or delays—or balances inventory: "Shift products from this region, they're selling like hotcakes in another." It's like a chess player, moving pieces smartly—coders feed it live GPS, sales, even news like "labor strike in this area." AI can be incredibly valuable in dynamic situations, catching unexpected spikes in demand before they cause problems.

For HR, it's fewer stressed teams; smoother chains mean calmer days. Job seekers can flex: "I'd use AI to cut delays!" It saves cash too—less stock sitting unsold in warehouses, more products reaching customers on time. It's not perfect—bad data (wrong truck logs) can misfire—but it's a lookahead lifeline. AI knows you'll want that product before you click, prepping it at the nearest hub. It's not just speed— it's smarts, untangling knots so goods glide, customers grin, and chaos shrinks to a blip.

34
What's one way AI can spot fake reviews online?

AI can sniff out fake reviews online like a hawk spotting a dodgy shadow—it's a sleuth for truth in the wild jungle of star ratings and gushing comments! One slick way it does this is by analysing how reviews are written, catching the "too good to be true" vibes that humans might miss. For service firms—like e-commerce or travel—it's a trust-builder, keeping feedback real.

Here's how: AI's trained on piles of reviews—legit ones from happy buyers and fakes from paid bots or grumpy rivals. It learns telltale signs. Say you're looking at a product online. A real review might say, "Works great, but a bit smaller than expected"—specific, balanced. A fake? "Best ever!!! Buy now!!!!"—over-the-top, vague, loaded with exclamation marks. AI spots this—it's got a nose for language patterns, like robotic repetition or hype that reeks of a script.

Take an example: a hotel gets 20 five-star "Amazing stay!" posts in an hour, all from new accounts. AI flags it—normal folks don't gush in sync like that. It's not just words; it checks timing, user history, even IP clusters—bots often pile on fast from one spot. AI might catch "same phrasing, different products" as a red flag, indicating suspicious activity.

Coders tweak it to weigh clues—short reviews score low, varied ones high. HR might use it to vet company buzz; job seekers can say, "I'd keep our rep clean!" It's not foolproof—clever fakes slip through, or legit rants get flagged—but it's a filter. AI sifts genuine feedback from suspicious posts, keeping trust alive. It's your online lie detector—sharp, not perfect, but a win for real vibes.

35
How music streaming apps make use of AI?

When a music streaming service picks your next song, it's AI working backstage, guessing your vibe like a DJ with a crystal ball! It's not random; it's a clever mix of your habits, crowd wisdom, and sound science, making your playlist feel like it gets you. For a service like this, it's all about keeping you hooked, one tune at a time.

Here's the trick: AI starts with your tracks—what you've played, skipped, or looped. Love a particular artist on repeat? It's noted. Skipped a slow track? It learns. It's trained on your history, plus millions of users'—think a giant music map. Say you're blasting popular hits. AI sees others with similar tastes often enjoy another artist next—it's a nudge: "Try this!" That's collaborative filtering, mixing your taste with the crowd's.

Then it dives deeper—into the music itself. AI breaks songs into bits—tempo, beats, mood—using audio analysis. "High energy, 120 BPM" might link one artist to another with a similar style, even if you've never heard them. It's not just names; it's sound DNA. It might catch a particular genre or regional vibe and suggest something new, expanding your musical horizons.

Coders tweak it—weight your "liked" songs over random skips. HR might see retention perks; job seekers can say, "I'd tune AI for users!" It's not perfect—skip a sad song once, and it might dodge ballads too long—but it adapts. Click "thumbs up," and it refines. It's your music shadow—blending what you love, what others do, and what sounds right—keeping the groove alive wherever you're vibing.

36
What's the role of testing in building an AI system?

Testing an AI system is like road-testing a car before you drive it—it's how you make sure it doesn't crash or take you to an unexpected destination! It's not a side gig; it's the backbone of building AI that works, catching hiccups so it's ready for the real world, whether it's for a service firm's chatbot or an HR hiring tool. Without it, you're flying blind.

Here's why it matters: AI learns from data—like past chats or sales—but that's just training. Testing checks if it's learned right. Say you're coding a chatbot for a telecom company—trained it on "recharge failed" complaints. You don't unleash it yet; you test it with fresh data: "My data's gone!" Does it reply "Top up here" or babble nonsense? You split data—train on 80%, test on 20%—so it's not just parroting, but solving new stuff.

It's a stress test too. Throw curveballs—like unexpected phrases or slang—and see if it fails. Different accents and slang can trip it up; testing finds those cracks. Coders measure it—accuracy (right answers), precision (no wild guesses)—tweaking till it sings. If it flags every call as "urgent," you've got a dud—testing shows that.

For HR, it's trust: "Will this AI pick fair hires?" Test it on diverse résumés—does it skip non-tech grads unfairly? Job seekers can flex: "I'd test AI for glitches!" It's not one-and-done—real-world use (like a live chatbot) feeds back, refining it more. Skip testing, and it's a gamble—imagine a retailer's AI predicting wildly inaccurate trends. Testing's your safety net—proving it's smart, not just shiny, before it meets the crowd.

37
What's the difference between AI and Machine Learning?

Many people use the terms AI and Machine Learning interchangeably, but there's a key difference. Think of AI as the big picture—the idea of creating machines that think like humans. Machine Learning is one tool in the AI toolbox, a specific way to achieve that goal.

Imagine a chef learning a new dish. AI is the goal—to cook delicious food. Machine Learning is like following a recipe—a specific method to achieve that goal. The chef (AI) uses the recipe (Machine Learning) to learn the steps, ingredients, and techniques needed to create the dish.

In more technical terms, Machine Learning is a type of AI that allows software applications to become more accurate in predicting outcomes without being explicitly programmed [1] to do so. It uses algorithms to analyse data, learn from it, and make informed decisions.

For example, a music streaming service using Machine Learning to recommend songs analyses your listening history, compares it to millions of other users, and predicts what you might enjoy next. The AI (the recommendation system) uses Machine Learning (analysing data and predicting preferences) to achieve its goal (keeping you grooving).

For HR, this distinction matters when discussing hiring tools or training programs. For a coder, it's about choosing the right technique for the task. Job seekers can show their understanding by saying, "I know Machine Learning is how we teach AI to learn from data." It's a subtle difference, but one that shows you understand the nuances of this exciting field.

38
How is AI changing the way we shop for groceries?

Gone are the days of wandering aimlessly through grocery aisles, wondering what to cook for dinner. AI is transforming grocery shopping into a personalized, efficient, and even enjoyable experience, both online and in physical stores.

Imagine this: you open your favourite grocery app, and it greets you with a list of suggested items based on your past purchases, dietary preferences, and even the current weather! Craving a warm soup on a rainy day? AI knows just the ingredients to recommend. Running low on milk? It reminds you to add it to your cart. It's like having a personal grocery assistant who anticipates your needs.

AI also powers those handy "frequently bought together" suggestions, reminding you to grab the naan to go with your butter chicken. This isn't just guesswork; it's based on analysing millions of transactions to see what items often land in the same basket. For those who prefer the in-store experience, AI is changing things there too. Smart shelves can track inventory in real-time, alerting staff when items are running low and even adjusting prices dynamically based on demand and expiration dates.

But it's not just about convenience. AI can also help you make healthier choices. By analysing your purchase history and dietary goals, it can suggest healthier alternatives or flag items that might not align with your wellness plan.

For those working in the grocery industry, this means adapting to new technologies and customer expectations. For consumers, it means a faster, more personalized shopping experience. And for job seekers, understanding how AI is reshaping retail can give you an edge in the job market. So next time you shop for groceries, remember that AI is working behind the scenes to make your experience smoother, smarter, and more satisfying.

39
How can AI help personalize education for students?

Imagine a classroom where every student learns at their own pace, focusing on the subjects they struggle with most, while a tireless AI tutor provides personalized support. This is the promise of AI in education – to create a learning experience that adapts to each student's unique needs and helps them reach their full potential.

Think of it like a personalized learning journey. AI can analyse a student's strengths and weaknesses, identify knowledge gaps, and tailor lessons accordingly. Struggling with algebra? AI can provide extra practice problems and targeted explanations. Excelling in history? It can offer more challenging material and suggest related topics for exploration.

AI can also provide valuable feedback to both students and teachers. By tracking progress and identifying areas where students are struggling, AI can alert teachers to intervene and provide additional support. This allows teachers to focus their attention where it's needed most, creating a more efficient and effective learning environment.

But it's not just about individualized learning. AI can also foster collaboration and create a more engaging learning experience. Imagine virtual study groups where AI connects students with similar learning styles or interests, or interactive simulations that bring historical events to life.

For educators, this means embracing new tools and adapting teaching methods. For students, it means a more personalized and engaging learning experience. And for job seekers in the education sector, understanding how AI can enhance learning can open up new opportunities and career paths. So, whether you're a student, teacher, or simply curious about the future of education, AI is poised to transform the way we learn and teach, creating a more personalized and effective experience for everyone.

40
How can AI help doctors diagnose diseases more accurately?

AI is becoming a powerful tool in the hands of doctors, helping them diagnose diseases with greater accuracy and speed. Imagine a world where medical diagnoses are faster, more accurate, and accessible to everyone, regardless of location or access to specialists. This is the potential of AI in healthcare.

Think of AI as a tireless assistant that can analyse vast amounts of medical data – patient records, lab results, medical images – and identify patterns that might be invisible to the human eye. For example, AI can analyse X-rays or scans to detect subtle anomalies that might indicate early signs of cancer or other diseases, often with greater accuracy than human experts.

AI can also help doctors make more informed treatment decisions. By analysing a patient's medical history, genetic information, and lifestyle factors, AI can predict how they might respond to different treatments and suggest the most effective course of action. This personalized approach to medicine can lead to better outcomes and improved patient care.

But it's not just about crunching data. AI can also help bridge the gap between patients and doctors, especially in remote areas with limited access to healthcare. Imagine a mobile app that uses AI to analyse symptoms and provide preliminary diagnoses, or a virtual assistant that can answer basic medical questions and schedule appointments.

For doctors, this means embracing new technologies and incorporating AI into their practice. For patients, it means faster, more accurate diagnoses and personalized treatment plans. And for job seekers in the healthcare industry, understanding how AI is transforming medicine can open up new career paths and opportunities. So, whether you're a doctor, patient, or simply curious about the future of healthcare, AI is poised to revolutionize the way we diagnose and treat diseases, creating a healthier future for everyone.

41
How can AI help us protect the environment?

AI is emerging as a powerful ally in the fight to protect our planet. From monitoring pollution to optimizing energy consumption, AI is helping us tackle some of the biggest environmental challenges facing our world.

Imagine a network of sensors constantly monitoring air and water quality, detecting pollution hotspots in real-time, and alerting authorities to take action. AI can analyse this data, identify sources of pollution, and even predict future environmental risks, allowing us to take proactive steps to protect our ecosystems.

AI can also help us use resources more efficiently. Think of smart grids that optimize energy distribution, reducing waste and lowering carbon emissions. Or AI-powered systems that analyse traffic patterns and optimize transportation routes, minimizing fuel consumption and congestion.

But it's not just about monitoring and optimization. AI can also help us develop innovative solutions to environmental problems. Imagine AI-powered robots cleaning up plastic waste in the oceans or AI algorithms designing more sustainable materials and products.

For those working in environmental science or conservation, this means embracing new technologies and incorporating AI into their research and fieldwork. For businesses, it means adopting AI-powered solutions to reduce their environmental footprint and contribute to a more sustainable future. And for job seekers, understanding how AI can be used to address environmental challenges can open up new career paths and opportunities. So, whether you're an environmentalist, a business leader, or simply someone who cares about the planet, AI is becoming an essential tool in our quest for a greener, more sustainable future.

42
How can AI make farming more efficient and sustainable?

AI is revolutionizing agriculture, helping farmers grow more food with fewer resources while minimizing their environmental impact. Imagine a world where farms are more efficient, productive, and sustainable, ensuring food security for a growing population while protecting our planet. This is the potential of AI in agriculture.

Think of AI-powered robots that can precisely plant seeds, monitor crop health, and even harvest crops autonomously, reducing the need for manual labour and minimizing waste. AI can analyse data from sensors, drones, and satellites to monitor soil conditions, water levels, and crop growth, providing farmers with real-time insights to optimize irrigation, fertilization, and pest control.

AI can also help farmers make more informed decisions about what to plant and when, based on factors like weather patterns, soil conditions, and market demand. This precision agriculture approach can help maximize yields while minimizing the use of resources like water and fertilizer.

But it's not just about increasing efficiency. AI can also help farmers adopt more sustainable practices. Imagine AI-powered systems that optimize water usage, reduce pesticide use, and even predict and prevent crop diseases, minimizing the environmental impact of agriculture.

For farmers, this means embracing new technologies and incorporating AI into their daily operations. For consumers, it means access to more affordable and sustainable food. And for job seekers in the agricultural sector, understanding how AI is transforming farming can open up new career paths and opportunities. So, whether you're a farmer, a consumer, or simply someone who cares about the future of food, AI is playing a crucial role in creating a more efficient, sustainable, and resilient agricultural system.

43
How is AI changing the way we travel and explore the world?

From personalized travel recommendations to self-driving cars and smart airports, AI is transforming the way we explore the world, making travel more efficient, enjoyable, and accessible to everyone.

Imagine planning your next vacation with the help of an AI-powered travel agent that knows your preferences better than you do! By analysing your past travel history, interests, and budget, AI can suggest destinations, create personalized itineraries, and even book flights and accommodations, taking the stress out of travel planning.

AI is also making travel safer and more efficient. Think of self-driving cars that navigate busy city streets or AI-powered systems that optimize traffic flow in airports and train stations, reducing delays and improving passenger experience.

But it's not just about convenience and efficiency. AI can also help us travel more sustainably. Imagine AI-powered apps that suggest eco-friendly transportation options, promote responsible tourism, and even help us offset our carbon footprint.

For those working in the travel and tourism industry, this means adapting to new technologies and incorporating AI into their services. For travellers, it means a more personalized, seamless, and sustainable travel experience. And for job seekers, understanding how AI is reshaping the travel industry can open up new career paths and opportunities. So, whether you're a seasoned globetrotter or planning your first adventure, AI is poised to revolutionize the way we travel and explore the world, making it easier, more enjoyable, and more accessible to everyone.

44
How can AI be used to create more personalized and engaging entertainment experiences?

AI is transforming the entertainment landscape, creating more personalized and immersive experiences for audiences. From recommending movies and music to generating interactive games and virtual reality worlds, AI is changing the way we consume and interact with entertainment.

Imagine an AI that curates a playlist of songs perfectly matched to your mood, or a movie recommendation system that understands your unique tastes better than any human critic. AI algorithms analyse your viewing and listening habits, preferences, and even your emotional state to deliver personalized recommendations that keep you engaged and entertained.

AI is also enabling the creation of entirely new forms of entertainment. Think of interactive video games where AI controls non-player characters that adapt to your playing style, or virtual reality experiences that respond to your movements and voice commands, creating a truly immersive and personalized adventure.

But it's not just about personalization. AI is also helping artists and creators push the boundaries of creativity. Imagine AI tools that can generate music, write scripts, or even create stunning visual effects, empowering artists to bring their visions to life in new and exciting ways.

For those working in the entertainment industry, this means embracing new technologies and exploring the creative possibilities of AI. For consumers, it means access to more personalized, engaging, and innovative entertainment experiences. And for job seekers, understanding how AI is reshaping the entertainment industry can open up new career paths and opportunities. So, whether you're a movie buff, a music lover, or a gamer, AI is poised to revolutionize the way we experience entertainment, making it more personal, interactive, and immersive than ever before.

45
How can AI help us combat fake news and misinformation online?

In today's digital age, where information spreads like wildfire, AI is emerging as a crucial tool in the fight against fake news and misinformation. From identifying fabricated content to verifying sources and debunking false claims, AI is helping us navigate the complex world of online information and make more informed decisions.

Imagine an AI-powered fact-checking system that can analyse news articles, social media posts, and even images and videos to detect inconsistencies, verify sources, and flag potentially false or misleading information. By cross-referencing information with trusted databases and identifying patterns of misinformation, AI can help us separate fact from fiction.

AI can also help us understand the spread of misinformation. By analysing social media networks and online communities, AI can identify how false narratives spread, who is responsible for creating and disseminating them, and how they impact public opinion. This can help us develop strategies to counter misinformation and promote more responsible online discourse.

But it's not just about detection and analysis. AI can also help us create more trustworthy sources of information. Imagine AI-powered news aggregators that prioritize credible sources and filter out unreliable content, or AI tools that help journalists verify information and create more accurate and unbiased reporting.

For those working in journalism, media, or online content creation, this means embracing new technologies and incorporating AI into their workflows. For consumers, it means access to more reliable information and a greater ability to make informed decisions. And for job seekers, understanding how AI can be used to combat misinformation can open up new career paths and opportunities. So, whether you're a journalist, a social media user, or simply someone who cares about the truth, AI is becoming an essential tool in the fight against fake news and misinformation, helping us create a more informed and responsible online world.

46
How can AI help us improve cybersecurity and protect our data?

With cyber threats becoming increasingly sophisticated, AI is emerging as a critical tool in the fight to protect our data and systems. From detecting malware to preventing phishing attacks and responding to security breaches, AI is helping us stay one step ahead of cybercriminals.

Imagine an AI-powered security system that can analyse network traffic, identify suspicious patterns, and detect malware and other threats in real-time, often before they can cause any damage. By learning from past attacks and adapting to new threats, AI can provide a dynamic and proactive defence against cyberattacks.

AI can also help us prevent phishing attacks and other social engineering scams. By analysing emails, messages, and websites for suspicious content and behaviour, AI can warn us of potential threats and help us avoid falling victim to scams.

But it's not just about prevention. AI can also help us respond to security breaches more effectively. By analysing attack patterns and identifying vulnerabilities, AI can help us contain breaches, minimize damage, and recover quickly.

For those working in cybersecurity or data protection, this means embracing new technologies and incorporating AI into their security strategies. For businesses, it means investing in AI-powered security solutions to protect their valuable data and systems. And for job seekers, understanding how AI is transforming cybersecurity can open up new career paths and opportunities. So, whether you're a security professional, a business owner, or simply someone who cares about online safety, AI is becoming an essential tool in the fight against cybercrime, helping us create a more secure and resilient digital world.

47
How can AI help us explore space and understand the universe?

AI is becoming an indispensable tool for space exploration, helping us analyse vast amounts of data, navigate complex environments, and even search for extraterrestrial life. From analysing astronomical data to controlling robotic explorers and designing future missions, AI is expanding our understanding of the cosmos.

Imagine an AI-powered telescope that can scan the skies for exoplanets, identify potentially habitable worlds, and even search for signs of extraterrestrial life. By analysing data from telescopes, satellites, and other instruments, AI can help us uncover the secrets of the universe and answer some of the biggest questions about our place in the cosmos.

AI is also playing a crucial role in robotic space exploration. Think of AI-powered rovers that can navigate the treacherous terrain of Mars, collect samples, and conduct experiments autonomously, providing us with valuable insights into the Red Planet and its potential for supporting life.

But it's not just about exploration and discovery. AI can also help us design more efficient and sustainable space missions. Imagine AI-powered systems that optimize spacecraft trajectories, reduce fuel consumption, and even design self-sustaining habitats for future space colonies.

For those working in astronomy, astrophysics, or space exploration, this means embracing new technologies and incorporating AI into their research and missions. For the rest of us, it means access to more exciting discoveries and a deeper understanding of the universe. And for job seekers, understanding how AI is transforming space exploration can open up new career paths and opportunities. So, whether you're a scientist, a space enthusiast, or simply curious about the cosmos, AI is poised to revolutionize our understanding of the universe and pave the way for future discoveries.

48
How can AI help us make better financial decisions?

AI is transforming the world of finance, helping us make smarter investment decisions, manage our money more effectively, and even prevent fraud. From personalized financial advice to automated trading and risk assessment, AI is changing the way we interact with money.

Imagine an AI-powered financial advisor that can analyse your income, expenses, and investment goals to create a personalized financial plan, suggest investment opportunities, and even automate your savings and investments. By tracking market trends, assessing risk, and learning from your financial behaviour, AI can help you make informed decisions and achieve your financial goals.

AI is also revolutionizing the way we invest. Think of AI-powered trading platforms that can analyse market data, identify trends, and execute trades autonomously, potentially outperforming human traders. AI can also help us assess risk more effectively, identifying potential investment pitfalls and protecting us from financial losses.

But it's not just about investing and wealth management. AI can also help us protect ourselves from fraud. Imagine AI-powered systems that can detect suspicious transactions, flag fraudulent activity, and even prevent identity theft, keeping our money safe and secure.

For those working in finance, this means adapting to new technologies and incorporating AI into their investment strategies and risk management processes. For consumers, it means access to more personalized financial advice, better investment opportunities, and greater financial security. And for job seekers, understanding how AI is transforming finance can open up new career paths and opportunities. So, whether you're a seasoned investor, a financial novice, or simply someone who wants to manage their money more effectively, AI is poised to revolutionize the way we interact with finance, making it more accessible, efficient, and secure.

49
How can AI help us create a more inclusive and accessible world for people with disabilities?

AI has the potential to break down barriers and create a more inclusive and accessible world for people with disabilities. From assistive technologies to personalized learning and accessible design, AI is empowering people with disabilities to live more independent and fulfilling lives.

Imagine an AI-powered wheelchair that can navigate complex environments, avoid obstacles, and even respond to voice commands, providing greater mobility and independence for people with physical disabilities. Or AI-powered screen readers that can convert text to speech, making online content accessible to people with visual impairments.

AI can also personalize learning experiences for students with disabilities. By analysing learning styles and adapting to individual needs, AI can help students with disabilities access education and achieve their full potential.

But it's not just about assistive technologies and education. AI can also promote accessibility in design and architecture. Imagine AI-powered tools that can analyse building plans and identify potential accessibility issues, or AI systems that can generate personalized accessibility solutions for individuals with different needs.

For those working in accessibility or disability services, this means embracing new technologies and incorporating AI into their support systems and assistive devices. For businesses and organizations, it means adopting AI-powered solutions to create more inclusive and accessible environments. And for job seekers, understanding how AI can promote accessibility can open up new career paths and opportunities. So, whether you're a person with a disability, an advocate, or simply someone who cares about creating a more inclusive world, AI is poised to play a crucial role in empowering people with disabilities and making our world more accessible to everyone.

50
How is AI changing the way we work and collaborate?

AI is transforming the workplace, automating tasks, enhancing productivity, and changing the way we collaborate. From intelligent assistants to collaborative robots and virtual meeting platforms, AI is reshaping the future of work.

Imagine an AI-powered assistant that can manage your schedule, prioritize your emails, and even generate reports, freeing you up to focus on more strategic and creative tasks. Or AI-powered tools that can translate languages in real-time, facilitating seamless communication and collaboration across borders.

AI is also changing the way we interact with technology in the workplace. Think of collaborative robots, or "cobots," that can work alongside humans in factories and warehouses, enhancing productivity and safety. Or AI-powered virtual meeting platforms that can transcribe conversations, generate summaries, and even analyse body language and facial expressions to provide insights into team dynamics.

But it's not just about automation and efficiency. AI can also foster a more inclusive and collaborative work environment. Imagine AI-powered tools that can identify and mitigate bias in hiring and promotion processes, or AI systems that can facilitate communication and collaboration among employees with diverse backgrounds and abilities.

For those already in the workforce, this means adapting to new technologies and developing new skills to work alongside AI. For job seekers, it means understanding how AI is changing the nature of work and preparing for the jobs of the future. And for businesses, it means embracing AI-powered solutions to enhance productivity, improve collaboration, and create a more inclusive and engaging workplace. So, whether you're an employee, a manager, or a business owner, AI is poised to revolutionize the way we work and collaborate, creating a more efficient, productive, and fulfilling work experience for everyone.

51
How can AI help us address global challenges like poverty and hunger?

AI has the potential to be a powerful force for good in the world, helping us tackle some of the most pressing global challenges, such as poverty and hunger. By analysing data, optimizing resources, and developing innovative solutions, AI can contribute to a more equitable and sustainable future for everyone.

Imagine AI-powered systems that can analyse poverty data, identify vulnerable populations, and target aid and resources where they are needed most. By understanding the root causes of poverty and predicting future trends, AI can help us develop more effective interventions and create a more equitable distribution of resources.

AI can also help us improve food security and combat hunger. Think of AI-powered systems that can analyse agricultural data, optimize crop yields, and predict and prevent food shortages. By improving efficiency and sustainability in agriculture, AI can help us ensure that everyone has access to nutritious food.

But it's not just about data analysis and optimization. AI can also help us develop innovative solutions to address global challenges. Imagine AI-powered tools that can provide education and healthcare services to remote and underserved communities, or AI systems that can empower marginalized groups and promote social inclusion.

For those working in international development, humanitarian aid, or social justice, this means embracing new technologies and incorporating AI into their programs and interventions. For governments and organizations, it means investing in AI-powered solutions to address global challenges and create a more equitable and sustainable world. And for job seekers, understanding how AI can be used to address social issues can open up new career paths and opportunities. So, whether you're a humanitarian worker, a policymaker, or simply someone who cares about making a difference in the world, AI is poised to play a crucial role in addressing global challenges and creating a more just and equitable future for everyone.

52
How can AI contribute to the development of smart cities?

AI is playing a crucial role in the development of smart cities, transforming urban environments into more efficient, sustainable, and liveable spaces. From optimizing traffic flow to improving public safety and enhancing citizen services, AI is making cities smarter and more responsive to the needs of their residents.

Imagine an AI-powered traffic management system that can analyse real-time traffic data, predict congestion hotspots, and optimize traffic flow, reducing commute times and improving air quality. Or AI-powered surveillance systems that can detect and prevent crime, enhancing public safety and creating a more secure urban environment.

AI can also improve the efficiency and sustainability of city services. Think of AI-powered waste management systems that can optimize garbage collection routes and predict waste generation patterns, reducing costs and minimizing environmental impact. Or AI-powered energy management systems that can optimize energy consumption in buildings and public spaces, reducing carbon emissions and promoting sustainability.

But it's not just about efficiency and sustainability. AI can also enhance citizen engagement and improve the quality of life in cities. Imagine AI-powered chatbots that can provide citizens with personalized information about city services, or AI-powered platforms that can facilitate citizen participation in urban planning and decision-making.

For city planners, urban designers, and government officials, this means embracing new technologies and incorporating AI into their urban development strategies. For citizens, it means living in more efficient, sustainable, and liveable cities. And for job seekers, understanding how AI is transforming urban environments can open up new career paths and opportunities. So, whether you're a city dweller, an urban planner, or simply someone who cares about the future of our cities, AI is poised to play a crucial role in creating smarter, more sustainable, and more liveable urban spaces for everyone.

53
How can AI help us create a more sustainable and efficient transportation system?

AI is revolutionizing transportation, making it more efficient, sustainable, and safe. From self-driving cars to smart traffic management systems and optimized logistics, AI is transforming the way we move people and goods.

Imagine a future where self-driving cars navigate our roads, reducing accidents and congestion, while optimizing fuel consumption and reducing emissions. AI can analyse real-time traffic data, predict traffic patterns, and optimize routes, making our commutes faster, safer, and more efficient.

AI is also transforming public transportation. Think of AI-powered bus and train scheduling systems that can adjust routes and frequencies in real-time based on passenger demand, reducing wait times and improving service reliability. Or AI-powered ride-sharing platforms that can match passengers with drivers, optimizing routes and reducing costs.

But it's not just about passenger transportation. AI is also optimizing logistics and supply chain management. Imagine AI-powered systems that can track shipments, predict delivery times, and optimize routes, reducing costs and improving efficiency.

For those working in transportation and logistics, this means embracing new technologies and incorporating AI into their operations. For commuters and travellers, it means faster, safer, and more sustainable transportation options. And for job seekers, understanding how AI is transforming transportation can open up new career paths and opportunities. So, whether you're a daily commuter, a logistics professional, or simply someone who cares about the future of transportation, AI is poised to play a crucial role in creating a more efficient, sustainable, and accessible transportation system for everyone.

54
How can AI help us personalize healthcare and improve patient outcomes?

AI is revolutionizing healthcare, enabling more personalized treatments, faster diagnoses, and improved patient outcomes. From analysing medical images to developing new drugs and providing personalized recommendations, AI is transforming the way we prevent, diagnose, and treat diseases.

Imagine an AI-powered system that can analyse your medical history, genetic information, and lifestyle factors to predict your risk of developing certain diseases and recommend personalized preventive measures. Or AI-powered diagnostic tools that can analyse medical images, identify subtle anomalies, and provide faster and more accurate diagnoses.

AI is also accelerating drug discovery and development. By analysing vast amounts of biomedical data, AI can identify promising drug candidates, predict their efficacy and safety, and even design personalized therapies tailored to individual patients.

But it's not just about technology. AI can also empower patients to take control of their own health. Imagine AI-powered apps that can track your symptoms, provide personalized health advice, and connect you with healthcare providers, enabling you to make informed decisions about your health.

For healthcare professionals, this means embracing new technologies and incorporating AI into their practice. For patients, it means access to more personalized and effective healthcare. And for job seekers in the healthcare industry, understanding how AI is transforming medicine can open up new career paths and opportunities. So, whether you're a doctor, a patient, or simply someone who cares about the future of healthcare, AI is poised to play a crucial role in creating a more personalized, precise, and proactive healthcare system for everyone.

55
How can AI help us personalize healthcare and improve patient outcomes?

AI is becoming a valuable tool for preserving and promoting cultural heritage, helping us protect historical artifacts, restore damaged artworks, and even revive lost languages. From digitizing ancient texts to creating interactive museum exhibits, AI is making cultural heritage more accessible and engaging for everyone.

Imagine an AI-powered system that can analyse historical documents, translate ancient languages, and even reconstruct damaged texts, preserving valuable cultural knowledge for future generations. Or AI-powered tools that can analyse and restore damaged artworks, bringing faded paintings and sculptures back to life.

AI can also help us create more engaging and interactive cultural experiences. Think of AI-powered museum exhibits that can provide personalized tours, answer visitor questions, and even recreate historical events in virtual reality, bringing the past to life in new and exciting ways.

But it's not just about preservation and restoration. AI can also help us discover and understand hidden connections between different cultures and historical periods. Imagine AI-powered systems that can analyse cultural artifacts, identify patterns and relationships, and uncover new insights into our shared human history.

For those working in museums, archives, and cultural institutions, this means embracing new technologies and incorporating AI into their preservation and research efforts. For the rest of us, it means access to a richer and more diverse cultural heritage. And for job seekers, understanding how AI can be used to preserve and promote culture can open up new career paths and opportunities. So, whether you're a historian, an artist, or simply someone who appreciates cultural heritage, AI is poised to play a crucial role in preserving our past and making it more accessible and engaging for everyone.

56
How can AI help us create a more just and equitable legal system?

AI is poised to transform the legal profession, making justice more accessible, efficient, and equitable. From analysing legal documents to predicting case outcomes and assisting with legal research, AI is changing the way lawyers work and how justice is served.

Imagine an AI-powered system that can analyse legal documents, identify relevant precedents, and even predict the outcome of a case, helping lawyers build stronger arguments and make more informed decisions. Or AI-powered tools that can automate legal research, freeing up lawyers to focus on more strategic tasks and provide better client service.

AI can also help address systemic biases in the legal system. By analysing data on sentencing patterns and legal outcomes, AI can identify and flag potential biases, promoting fairness and equality in the application of the law.

But it's not just about efficiency and fairness. AI can also make legal services more accessible to everyone. Imagine AI-powered chatbots that can provide basic legal advice, answer common legal questions, and even assist with legal document preparation, making legal assistance more affordable and accessible to those who need it most.

For lawyers and legal professionals, this means embracing new technologies and incorporating AI into their practice. For citizens, it means access to more efficient, affordable, and equitable legal services. And for job seekers in the legal field, understanding how AI is transforming the legal profession can open up new career paths and opportunities. So, whether you're a lawyer, a judge, or simply someone who cares about justice, AI is poised to play a crucial role in creating a more just, efficient, and equitable legal system for everyone.

57
How can AI help us improve disaster preparedness and response?

AI is becoming an invaluable tool for disaster preparedness and response, helping us predict, mitigate, and respond to natural disasters more effectively. From analysing weather patterns to coordinating emergency response efforts and providing real-time information to affected communities, AI is saving lives and minimizing the impact of disasters.

Imagine an AI-powered system that can analyse weather data, predict the path of a hurricane or the likelihood of a flood, and provide early warnings to vulnerable communities, enabling them to evacuate or take other protective measures. Or AI-powered drones that can assess damage after a disaster, identify survivors, and deliver essential supplies to those in need.

AI can also help coordinate emergency response efforts. Think of AI-powered platforms that can connect first responders with those in need, optimize evacuation routes, and allocate resources efficiently, ensuring a swift and effective response to disasters.

But it's not just about prediction and response. AI can also help us mitigate the impact of disasters. Imagine AI-powered systems that can analyse building designs and infrastructure to identify vulnerabilities and recommend improvements, making our communities more resilient to natural disasters.

For those working in disaster relief, emergency management, and urban planning, this means embracing new technologies and incorporating AI into their preparedness and response strategies. For communities at risk, it means greater safety and resilience in the face of natural disasters. And for job seekers, understanding how AI can be used to improve disaster preparedness and response can open up new career paths and opportunities. So, whether you're a first responder, a community leader, or simply someone who cares about disaster preparedness, AI is poised to play a crucial role in helping us create a more resilient and prepared world.

58
How can AI help us create a more efficient and sustainable manufacturing industry?

AI is transforming manufacturing, making it more efficient, sustainable, and competitive. From optimizing production processes to improving quality control and enabling predictive maintenance, AI is revolutionizing the factory floor.

Imagine an AI-powered system that can analyse production data, identify bottlenecks, and optimize workflows, improving efficiency and reducing waste. Or AI-powered robots that can work alongside humans on the assembly line, performing tasks that are dangerous or repetitive, improving productivity and safety.

AI can also enhance quality control in manufacturing. Think of AI-powered vision systems that can inspect products for defects with greater accuracy and speed than human inspectors, ensuring that only high-quality products reach consumers.

But it's not just about efficiency and quality. AI can also make manufacturing more sustainable. Imagine AI-powered systems that can optimize energy consumption, reduce waste, and even design more environmentally friendly products and processes.

For manufacturers, this means embracing new technologies and incorporating AI into their production processes. For consumers, it means access to higher quality, more affordable, and more sustainable products. And for job seekers in the manufacturing industry, understanding how AI is transforming the factory floor can open up new career paths and opportunities. So, whether you're a factory worker, a production manager, or simply someone who cares about the future of manufacturing, AI is poised to play a crucial role in creating a more efficient, sustainable, and competitive manufacturing industry.

59
How can AI help us bridge the digital divide and promote digital literacy?

AI has the potential to bridge the digital divide and promote digital literacy, making technology more accessible and empowering for everyone, regardless of their background or location. From personalized learning platforms to AI-powered translation tools and accessible user interfaces, AI is breaking down barriers to digital inclusion.

Imagine an AI-powered learning platform that can adapt to individual learning styles, provide personalized instruction, and offer support in multiple languages, making digital skills accessible to everyone, including those in underserved communities and those with disabilities. Or AI-powered translation tools that can break down language barriers and make online content accessible to people around the world.

AI can also help us design more accessible and user-friendly technology. Think of AI-powered interfaces that can adapt to individual needs and preferences, making technology easier to use for people with disabilities and older adults.

But it's not just about access and usability. AI can also promote digital literacy by providing personalized guidance and support. Imagine AI-powered mentors that can guide users through online resources, answer questions, and provide feedback, helping them develop essential digital skills.

For educators, policymakers, and community leaders, this means embracing new technologies and incorporating AI into their digital inclusion strategies. For individuals, it means access to the tools and resources they need to thrive in the digital age. And for job seekers, understanding how AI can promote digital literacy can open up new career paths and opportunities. So, whether you're a student, a teacher, or simply someone who wants to improve their digital skills, AI is poised to play a crucial role in bridging the digital divide and creating a more inclusive and equitable digital world.

60
How can AI help us improve public safety and reduce crime?

AI is transforming law enforcement and public safety, helping us prevent crime, improve emergency response times, and create safer communities. From predictive policing to facial recognition technology and AI-powered surveillance systems, AI is changing the way we protect our cities and citizens.

Imagine an AI-powered system that can analyse crime data, identify patterns, and predict where and when crimes are likely to occur, allowing law enforcement to allocate resources more effectively and prevent crimes before they happen. Or AI-powered surveillance systems that can detect suspicious activity, identify potential threats, and alert authorities in real-time, enhancing public safety and reducing response times.

AI can also help us improve the efficiency and accuracy of investigations. Think of AI-powered facial recognition technology that can identify suspects in crowds or analyse video footage to track down criminals. Or AI-powered tools that can analyse crime scenes, identify evidence, and even reconstruct events, helping investigators solve crimes more quickly and effectively.

But it's not just about prevention and investigation. AI can also help us address the root causes of crime. Imagine AI-powered systems that can identify at-risk individuals and communities, provide early interventions, and connect people with resources and support, helping to prevent crime and promote social inclusion.

For law enforcement agencies, this means embracing new technologies and incorporating AI into their crime prevention and investigation strategies. For citizens, it means living in safer communities. And for job seekers in the law enforcement and security fields, understanding how AI is transforming public safety can open up new career paths and opportunities. So, whether you're a police officer, a community leader, or simply someone who cares about public safety, AI is poised to play a crucial role in creating safer and more secure communities for everyone.

61
How can AI help us understand and address the challenges of aging populations?

AI is emerging as a valuable tool in addressing the challenges and opportunities presented by aging populations around the world. From providing personalized healthcare to developing assistive technologies and fostering social inclusion, AI can help older adults live longer, healthier, and more fulfilling lives.

Imagine AI-powered systems that can analyse health data, predict age-related health risks, and recommend personalized preventive measures, helping older adults maintain their independence and well-being. Or AI-powered assistive technologies that can provide support with daily tasks, such as medication management, mobility, and communication, enabling older adults to live more independently in their own homes.

AI can also help address social isolation and loneliness among older adults. Think of AI-powered companion robots that can provide social interaction and emotional support, or AI-powered platforms that can connect older adults with friends, family, and community resources.

But it's not just about healthcare and social support. AI can also help older adults stay active and engaged in their communities. Imagine AI-powered learning platforms that can provide personalized educational opportunities, or AI-powered tools that can help older adults find volunteer opportunities and contribute their skills and experience to society.

For healthcare providers, caregivers, and policymakers, this means embracing new technologies and incorporating AI into their aging-in-place strategies and support systems. For older adults, it means access to personalized care, greater independence, and a higher quality of life. And for job seekers, understanding how AI can be used to address the challenges of aging populations can open up new career paths and opportunities. So, whether you're a healthcare professional, a caregiver, or simply someone who cares about the well-being of older adults, AI is poised to play a crucial role in creating a more age-friendly and inclusive society.

62
How can AI help us improve mental health care and support?

AI is emerging as a valuable tool in improving mental health care and providing support to those who need it most. From early detection and diagnosis to personalized treatment and ongoing support, AI is transforming the way we approach mental health.

Imagine an AI-powered system that can analyse social media posts, text messages, and even voice patterns to detect early signs of mental health conditions like depression or anxiety, enabling timely intervention and support. Or AI-powered chatbots that can provide immediate support and guidance to those in crisis, offering a safe and accessible space to talk about their mental health.

AI can also personalize mental health treatment. Think of AI-powered platforms that can recommend therapy approaches, track progress, and even provide personalized feedback and encouragement, helping individuals achieve their mental health goals.

But it's not just about technology. AI can also help reduce stigma and promote mental health awareness. Imagine AI-powered campaigns that can educate the public about mental health, challenge misconceptions, and encourage people to seek help when they need it.

For mental health professionals, this means embracing new technologies and incorporating AI into their practice. For individuals struggling with mental health challenges, it means access to more personalized and accessible support. And for job seekers in the mental health field, understanding how AI is transforming mental health care can open up new career paths and opportunities. So, whether you're a therapist, a patient, or simply someone who cares about mental health, AI is poised to play a crucial role in creating a more supportive and inclusive mental health care system for everyone.

63
How can AI help us make scientific discoveries and advance research?

AI is accelerating scientific discovery and innovation, helping researchers analyse vast amounts of data, identify patterns, and generate new hypotheses. From drug discovery to materials science and climate modelling, AI is transforming the way we conduct research and pushing the boundaries of human knowledge.

Imagine an AI-powered system that can analyse scientific literature, identify research gaps, and suggest promising areas for further investigation. Or AI-powered tools that can analyse experimental data, identify patterns and anomalies, and generate new hypotheses, accelerating the pace of scientific discovery.

AI is also enabling new forms of scientific collaboration. Think of AI-powered platforms that can connect researchers from around the world, facilitate data sharing, and promote interdisciplinary collaboration, leading to breakthroughs in fields ranging from medicine to environmental science.

But it's not just about data analysis and collaboration. AI can also help us design and conduct experiments more efficiently. Imagine AI-powered systems that can optimize experimental parameters, automate data collection, and even control laboratory equipment, freeing up researchers to focus on more creative and strategic tasks.

For scientists and researchers, this means embracing new technologies and incorporating AI into their research workflows. For society as a whole, it means access to new discoveries and innovations that can improve our lives and address global challenges. And for job seekers in the scientific and research fields, understanding how AI is transforming science can open up new career paths and opportunities. So, whether you're a scientist, a researcher, or simply someone who is curious about the world around us, AI is poised to play a crucial role in accelerating scientific discovery and advancing human knowledge.

64
How can AI help improve customer service in a call centre environment?

AI can significantly enhance customer service in a call centre by automating tasks, personalizing interactions, and providing agents with valuable insights. This leads to faster resolution times, increased customer satisfaction, and reduced operational costs.

Imagine an AI-powered chatbot that can handle basic customer queries in multiple languages, providing instant support and freeing up human agents to handle more complex issues. This not only reduces wait times but also caters to a diverse customer base.

AI can also personalize customer interactions by analysing past interactions and customer data to provide agents with relevant information and recommendations. This enables agents to offer tailored solutions and build stronger relationships with customers.

Furthermore, AI can analyse customer sentiment in real-time, alerting agents to potential issues and providing them with the information they need to de-escalate situations and provide proactive support. This can help improve customer satisfaction and reduce churn.

For a call centre, this means improved efficiency, happier customers, and a more engaged workforce. As a job seeker, I can highlight my understanding of how AI can be used to enhance customer service and contribute to a company's success.

This version keeps the core ideas while removing the India-specific mention, making it applicable to a wider range of call centre settings.

65
How can AI be used to improve the efficiency and accuracy of data entry tasks in a service-based company?

AI can significantly improve the efficiency and accuracy of data entry tasks in a service-based company by automating processes, reducing manual errors, and freeing up employees for more complex tasks. This leads to increased productivity, improved data quality, and reduced operational costs.

Imagine an AI-powered system that can automatically extract data from documents, such as invoices, forms, and emails, and populate databases with minimal human intervention. This eliminates the need for manual data entry, reducing errors and saving valuable time.

AI can also be used to validate and clean data, identifying inconsistencies, errors, and duplicates. This ensures that the data used by the company is accurate and reliable, which is crucial for making informed decisions and providing quality service to clients.

Furthermore, AI can learn from past data entry patterns and suggest corrections or improvements, further enhancing accuracy and efficiency. This can help employees avoid common mistakes and improve their overall performance.

For a service-based company, this means streamlined operations, improved data quality, and increased employee satisfaction. As a job seeker, I can highlight my understanding of how AI can be used to optimize data entry processes and contribute to a company's efficiency and productivity.

66
How can AI be used to enhance training and development programs for employees in a service-based company?

AI can revolutionize employee training and development programs in a service-based company by personalizing learning experiences, providing targeted feedback, and optimizing training content for better knowledge retention and skill development.

Imagine an AI-powered learning platform that can assess an employee's strengths and weaknesses, identify skill gaps, and recommend personalized training modules and resources. This ensures that employees receive training that is relevant to their individual needs and helps them develop the skills they need to excel in their roles.

AI can also provide real-time feedback and guidance during training simulations and assessments, helping employees learn from their mistakes and improve their performance. This personalized feedback can be more effective than traditional training methods, which often rely on generic feedback or delayed evaluations.

Furthermore, AI can analyse training data to identify areas where employees are struggling and recommend improvements to the training content and delivery methods. This ensures that the training program is constantly evolving and adapting to the needs of the employees.

For a service-based company, this means a more engaged and skilled workforce, leading to improved customer satisfaction and better business outcomes. As a job seeker, I can emphasize my understanding of how AI can be used to create more effective training programs and contribute to employee development and success.

67
How can AI be used to improve project management and collaboration in a service-based company?

AI can significantly enhance project management and collaboration in a service-based company by automating tasks, predicting risks, and facilitating communication, leading to more efficient project delivery and improved team performance.

Imagine an AI-powered project management tool that can analyse project data, predict potential delays or roadblocks, and recommend proactive measures to mitigate risks. This can help project managers stay ahead of schedule and avoid costly setbacks.

AI can also facilitate communication and collaboration among team members by providing a centralized platform for sharing information, tracking progress, and coordinating tasks. This can help improve team efficiency and reduce communication breakdowns.

Furthermore, AI can automate routine project management tasks, such as scheduling meetings, generating reports, and assigning tasks, freeing up project managers to focus on more strategic activities.

For a service-based company, this means improved project outcomes, increased efficiency, and better collaboration among teams. As a job seeker, I can highlight my understanding of how AI can be used to optimize project management processes and contribute to a company's success.

68
How can AI be used to optimize pricing strategies and improve profitability in a service-based company?

AI can help service-based companies optimize their pricing strategies by analysing market trends, customer behaviour, and competitor pricing to identify the optimal price points for their services. This can lead to increased revenue, improved profitability, and a competitive advantage in the marketplace.

Imagine an AI-powered pricing tool that can analyse historical data, predict demand, and recommend optimal pricing adjustments based on various factors, such as time of day, customer segment, and competitor activity. This dynamic pricing approach can help companies maximize revenue and profitability.

AI can also analyse customer data to identify price sensitivity and willingness to pay, enabling companies to tailor their pricing strategies to different customer segments. This can help companies attract and retain customers while maximizing revenue.

Furthermore, AI can monitor competitor pricing in real-time, providing companies with valuable insights to adjust their pricing strategies and stay ahead of the competition.

For a service-based company, this means optimized pricing, increased revenue, and improved profitability. As a job seeker, I can demonstrate my understanding of how AI can be used to enhance pricing strategies and contribute to a company's financial success.

69
How can AI be used to identify and mitigate risks in a service-based company?

AI can play a crucial role in identifying and mitigating risks in a service-based company by analysing data, predicting potential threats, and providing insights to help companies make informed decisions and proactively manage risks.

Imagine an AI-powered system that can analyse customer data, financial transactions, and operational processes to identify potential risks, such as fraud, security breaches, and operational disruptions. By identifying patterns and anomalies, AI can alert companies to potential threats and enable them to take proactive measures to mitigate risks.

AI can also be used to predict the likelihood of future risks based on historical data and current trends. This predictive capability can help companies anticipate potential challenges and develop strategies to minimize their impact.

Furthermore, AI can provide valuable insights into the effectiveness of risk mitigation strategies, enabling companies to continuously improve their risk management processes.

For a service-based company, this means enhanced risk management, improved decision-making, and greater resilience in the face of uncertainty. As a job seeker, I can highlight my understanding of how AI can be used to identify and mitigate risks and contribute to a company's overall stability and success.

70
Imagine you're explaining AI to your grandparents. How would you describe "computer vision" in a way they could understand?

I'd tell my grandparents that computer vision is like giving a computer a pair of eyes so it can "see" and understand the world around it, just like we do. But instead of using eyes, it uses cameras and clever algorithms to analyse images and videos.

For example, I'd say, "Imagine you're looking at a photo of our family. You can easily recognize everyone in the picture, right? Computer vision allows a computer to do the same thing. It can identify faces, objects, and even emotions in images."

I'd also give them some real-world examples that they can relate to. "Have you seen those self-driving cars? They use computer vision to 'see' the road, other cars, and pedestrians, allowing them to navigate safely. Or those apps that can identify plants and flowers just by taking a picture? That's computer vision at work too!"

By using simple language and relatable examples, I can help my grandparents understand this complex concept and appreciate the potential of AI to improve our lives.

71
You're teaching a beginner's coding class. How would you explain the concept of a "neural network" in a simple and engaging way?

Think of a neural network like a team of detectives working together to solve a mystery. Each detective (or "neuron" in a neural network) has a specific clue or piece of information. They pass these clues around, sharing and combining them until they have enough evidence to crack the case.

In a neural network, these clues are numbers and the detectives are simple mathematical functions. The network learns by adjusting the connections between the neurons, strengthening those that lead to the right answer and weakening those that don't.

For example, imagine you're teaching a neural network to recognize cats in pictures. You'd show it tons of pictures of cats and other animals. Each neuron might focus on a different feature, like pointy ears, whiskers, or a furry tail. By sharing and combining these features, the network learns to identify what makes a cat a cat.

It's like a game of "telephone" where the message gets clearer with each whisper. The more data you feed the network, the better it gets at solving the mystery and making accurate predictions.

This simple analogy can help beginners grasp the basic idea of a neural network and its ability to learn from data, without getting bogged down in complex mathematics.

72
Explain the concept of "overfitting" in machine learning to someone with no technical background, using a simple analogy.

Imagine you're teaching a child to recognize different types of flowers. You show them pictures of roses, lilies, and sunflowers, and they quickly learn to identify them. But then, you only show them pictures of red roses for a week. When you suddenly show them a yellow rose, they might not recognize it as a rose because they've "overfit" their understanding of roses to only include red ones.

Overfitting in machine learning is similar. It happens when an AI model learns the training data too well, including all the little details and quirks, and fails to generalize to new, unseen data. It's like memorizing the answers to a test instead of understanding the concepts.

In the real world, this could mean a fraud detection system that's trained on old scams might miss new types of fraud, or a customer service chatbot that's trained on formal language might struggle with slang or colloquialisms.

To avoid overfitting, we need to make sure the AI model is exposed to a diverse range of data and that it doesn't get too attached to the specifics of the training data. It's like teaching the child about different colours and shapes of roses, so they can recognize a rose no matter what it looks like.

This simple analogy can help explain a complex concept like overfitting in a way that anyone can understand, highlighting the importance of balanced and diverse data for building effective AI models.

73
Explain the difference between "classification" and "regression" in machine learning to a non-technical audience, using everyday examples.

Imagine you're sorting a basket of fruits. You can classify them into different categories, like apples, oranges, and bananas. This is similar to classification in machine learning, where the AI model learns to categorize data into different groups or classes.

For example, a spam filter classifies emails as either "spam" or "not spam," or a medical diagnosis system classifies patients as "healthy" or "sick."

Now, imagine you're trying to predict the price of a house. You might consider factors like its size, location, and age. This is similar to regression in machine learning, where the AI model learns to predict a continuous value, like price, temperature, or stock market trends.

For example, a weather forecasting app uses regression to predict the temperature for the next day, or a food delivery app uses regression to estimate the delivery time based on distance and traffic conditions.

In simple terms, classification is like sorting things into buckets, while regression is like drawing a line to predict a value. Both are powerful tools in machine learning, used in various applications to solve different types of problems.

This simple explanation, using everyday examples, can help a non-technical audience understand the difference between these two fundamental concepts in machine learning.

74
Explain the concept of "data bias" in AI to someone with no technical background, using a relatable analogy.

Imagine you're baking a cake, but you only have a recipe for chocolate cake. You try to bake a vanilla cake using the same recipe, but it doesn't turn out right. That's because the recipe is biased towards chocolate cake.

Data bias in AI is similar. It happens when the data used to train an AI model is not representative of the real world, leading to inaccurate or unfair predictions.

For example, if a facial recognition system is trained mostly on images of people with lighter skin tones, it might have difficulty recognizing people with darker skin tones. This is because the data is biased towards a particular group of people.

Similarly, if a loan approval system is trained on data that reflects historical biases in lending practices, it might unfairly discriminate against certain groups of applicants.

To avoid data bias, it's important to use diverse and representative data that reflects the real world. It's like having a recipe book with recipes for all sorts of cakes, so you can bake the perfect cake no matter what flavour you choose.

This simple analogy can help explain a complex concept like data bias in a way that anyone can understand, highlighting the importance of using fair and unbiased data for building ethical and effective AI systems.

75
You're explaining AI to a group of children. How would you describe "natural language processing" in a way they could understand and find interesting?

Imagine you have a magic wand that can understand anything you say, no matter how you say it! That's kind of like natural language processing, or NLP. It's like teaching computers to understand and talk like humans.

Think of your favourite voice assistant, like Siri or Alexa. When you ask it to play a song or tell you the weather, it uses NLP to understand what you mean, even if you say it in different ways. It's like having a friend who can understand you, even if you mumble or use slang!

NLP also helps computers do cool things like translate languages, write stories, and even have conversations with you. It's like having a superpower that lets you talk to anyone in the world or create your own stories with the help of a computer.

So, next time you talk to your phone or computer, remember that NLP is the magic behind it, making it possible for machines to understand and communicate with us in a way that feels natural and fun!

76
As a developer, how would you approach choosing the right machine learning algorithm for a specific problem? What factors would you consider?

When selecting a machine learning algorithm, I'd consider several key factors to ensure the chosen algorithm aligns with the problem's requirements and the available data. It's not a one-size-fits-all approach, and careful consideration is crucial for optimal results. Here's my approach:

1. **Understanding the Problem:**

- **Type of problem:** Is it a classification, regression, clustering, or dimensionality reduction task? The problem type significantly narrows down the suitable algorithm choices.
- **Business goals:** What are the specific objectives? Accuracy, speed, interpretability, or scalability might be prioritized differently depending on the business context.
- **Data availability:** How much labelled data is available? Some algorithms thrive on large datasets, while others perform better with limited data.

2. **Analysing the Data:**

- **Data type:** Is it numerical, categorical, textual, or a combination? Different algorithms are designed for different data types.
- **Data size:** Is the dataset small, medium, or large? Scalability is a major concern for large datasets.
- **Data quality:** Are there missing values, outliers, or noisy data? Data preprocessing techniques and algorithm robustness become important considerations.
- **Data distribution:** Is the data linearly separable? Is there class imbalance? The data distribution can influence algorithm performance.

3. **Evaluating Algorithm Characteristics:**

- **Complexity:** How computationally expensive is the algorithm? Training time and prediction time are crucial for real-time applications.
- **Interpretability:** How easy is it to understand the model's decision-making process? This is vital in regulated industries or when trust and transparency are paramount.
- **Accuracy:** What is the expected performance on unseen data? This is typically measured using metrics like precision, recall, F1-score, or RMSE.
- **Robustness:** How well does the algorithm handle noisy data or outliers?
- **Scalability:** How well does the algorithm perform as the dataset size grows?

4. **Experimentation and Evaluation:**

- **Try multiple algorithms:** Start with a few promising algorithms and compare their performance on a validation set.
- **Use appropriate evaluation metrics:** Choose metrics that align with the business goals and the problem type.
- **Tune hyperparameters:** Optimize the algorithm's parameters to achieve the best possible performance.
- **Cross-validation:** Use techniques like k-fold cross-validation to get a more reliable estimate of the algorithm's performance.

5. **Practical Considerations:**

- **Library and tool support:** Are there well-maintained and efficient implementations of the algorithm available?
- **Community support:** Is there a large and active community that can provide help and resources?
- **Deployment requirements:** What are the requirements for deploying the model In a production environment?

By carefully considering these factors, I can make an informed decision and select the most appropriate machine learning algorithm for a given problem.

77
Explain the concept of "regularization" in machine learning to a non-technical audience, using a simple analogy.

Imagine you're trying to learn a new dance routine. You practice the steps over and over again, but you start adding your own little flourishes and improvisations. While it might look fancy, you might forget the original steps and mess up the whole routine during the performance.

Regularization in machine learning is like a dance instructor who keeps you from getting too fancy. It prevents the AI model from learning the training data too well, which can lead to overfitting and poor performance on new data.

Think of it like adding a penalty for every extra step or flourish you add to the dance routine. This encourages the model to focus on the essential steps and avoid memorizing the specific details of the training data.

In simpler terms, regularization helps the AI model find a balance between learning the patterns in the data and keeping things simple enough to generalize to new situations. It's like learning the basic steps of the dance so well that you can perform it flawlessly, even with a different partner or on a different stage.

This simple analogy can help explain a complex concept like regularization in a way that anyone can understand, highlighting its importance in building robust and reliable AI models.

78

How would you explain the difference between "supervised learning," "unsupervised learning," and "reinforcement learning" to someone with no technical background, using real-world examples?

Imagine you're teaching a dog new trick. You can use different approaches depending on the trick and the dog's personality.

Supervised learning is like teaching the dog to "sit" by giving it a treat every time it sits on command. You're providing the dog with clear instructions and feedback, guiding it towards the desired behaviour. In machine learning, this is like giving the AI model labelled data, where the correct answer is provided for each example.

Unsupervised learning is like observing the dog playing in the park and noticing that it likes to chase squirrels. You didn't give it any specific instructions, but it learned to identify and chase squirrels on its own by exploring its environment. In machine learning, this is like giving the AI model unlabelled data and letting it discover patterns and relationships on its own.

Reinforcement learning is like teaching the dog to fetch a ball by giving it positive reinforcement (like praise or a treat) when it brings the ball back and negative reinforcement (like ignoring it) when it doesn't. The dog learns through trial and error, adjusting its behaviour based on the feedback it receives. In machine learning, this is like letting the AI model interact with an environment and learn by receiving rewards or penalties for its actions.

These different learning approaches are used in various AI applications. For example, supervised learning is used for image recognition and spam filtering, unsupervised learning is used for customer segmentation and anomaly detection, and reinforcement learning is used for game playing and robotics.

This simple analogy, using a relatable example like dog training, can help explain the differences between these three fundamental learning paradigms in machine learning.

79
What are some common challenges faced when deploying machine learning models in a production environment, and how would you address them?

Deploying machine learning models in a production environment can be challenging due to various factors, including data dependencies, infrastructure limitations, and the need for continuous monitoring and maintenance. Here are some common challenges and how I would address them:

1. Data Dependencies and Drift:

- **Challenge:** Models are trained on historical data, which may not reflect the real-world data distribution in a production environment. This can lead to performance degradation over time as the data drifts.
- **Solution:** Implement data validation and monitoring pipelines to track data quality and identify potential drift. Retrain models periodically with fresh data or use techniques like online learning to adapt to changing data distributions.

2. Infrastructure Limitations:

- **Challenge:** Deploying and scaling machine learning models can require significant computational resources and infrastructure, which can be expensive and complex to manage.
- **Solution:** Optimize models for efficiency and consider using cloud-based infrastructure or serverless computing platforms to scale resources as needed.

3. Model Monitoring and Maintenance:

- **Challenge:** Models can degrade over time due to changes in data distribution or the emergence of new patterns. Continuous monitoring and maintenance are crucial to ensure optimal performance.

- **Solution:** Implement monitoring dashboards to track model performance metrics and alert for potential issues. Establish a process for retraining or updating models as needed, and consider using techniques like A/B testing to evaluate new model versions.

4. Model Explainability and Interpretability:

- **Challenge:** Complex machine learning models can be difficult to understand and interpret, making it challenging to debug issues or explain predictions to stakeholders.
- **Solution:** Use techniques like SHAP values or LIME to explain model predictions and identify important features. Consider using simpler models or rule-based systems when interpretability is critical.

5. Security and Privacy:

- **Challenge:** Machine learning models can be vulnerable to security threats and privacy breaches, especially when dealing with sensitive data.
- **Solution:** Implement security measures to protect models and data, such as encryption, access control, and regular security audits. Ensure compliance with data privacy regulations like GDPR.

By proactively addressing these challenges, I can ensure the successful deployment and maintenance of machine learning models in a production environment, delivering value to the business and its customers.

80
Explain the concept of "transfer learning" in machine learning to a non-technical audience, using a simple analogy.

Imagine you're learning to play the piano. You start by learning the basic scales and chords, which takes time and effort. But once you've mastered those fundamentals, you can easily apply that knowledge to learn new songs. You don't have to start from scratch every time.

Transfer learning in machine learning is similar. It's like taking the knowledge gained from solving one problem and applying it to a different but related problem. This can save time and resources, as the AI model doesn't have to learn everything from scratch.

For example, imagine an AI model that's been trained to recognize different types of cars. This model can then be fine-tuned to recognize different types of trucks, as the knowledge about shapes, wheels, and other features is transferable.

In the real world, transfer learning is used in various applications, such as image recognition, natural language processing, and speech recognition. For example, a pre-trained image recognition model can be fine-tuned to identify specific objects, like medical images or satellite imagery.

This simple analogy can help explain a complex concept like transfer learning in a way that anyone can understand, highlighting its potential to accelerate AI development and solve new problems more efficiently.

81
What is the difference between "batch learning" and "online learning" in machine learning, and when would you choose one over the other?

Imagine you're learning a new language. You can choose to learn in a batch, like taking a course with a fixed curriculum and schedule, or you can learn online, picking up new words and phrases as you go, adapting to your own pace and needs.

Batch learning in machine learning is like the classroom approach. The AI model is trained on a fixed dataset, learning all at once, and then deployed to make predictions. This is suitable for problems where the data is relatively static and doesn't change frequently, like image recognition or spam filtering.

Online learning, on the other hand, is like the continuous learning approach. The AI model learns incrementally, updating its knowledge as new data becomes available. This is suitable for problems where the data is dynamic and changes frequently, like stock market prediction or fraud detection.

Choosing between batch learning and online learning depends on the specific problem and the characteristics of the data. Batch learning is simpler and more efficient for static data, while online learning is more adaptable and responsive to dynamic data.

For example, a batch learning approach might be suitable for training a customer churn prediction model using historical data, while an online learning approach might be more appropriate for a fraud detection system that needs to adapt to new fraud patterns in real-time.

Understanding the difference between these two learning paradigms can help developers choose the right approach for their specific needs and build more effective AI solutions.

82
How would you explain the concept of "A/B testing" in the context of machine learning to someone with no technical background?

Imagine you're a chef trying out a new recipe for a pizza. You make two versions: one with the original recipe and another with a slightly different sauce. You then offer both pizzas to your customers and observe which one they prefer.

A/B testing in machine learning is similar. It's like comparing two versions of an AI model to see which one performs better. You split your audience into two groups, show one group the original model (version A) and the other group the modified model (version B), and then track which one achieves better results.

For example, you might A/B test different versions of a product recommendation system on an e-commerce website to see which one leads to more sales, or you might test different versions of a chatbot to see which one leads to higher customer satisfaction.

The key is to make only one change at a time, so you can isolate the impact of that change on the model's performance. This allows you to make data-driven decisions about which model to deploy and how to improve its effectiveness.

A/B testing is a powerful tool for optimizing machine learning models and ensuring that they deliver the best possible results. It's like a scientific experiment that helps you fine-tune your AI recipe for success.

83
What is the importance of "feature engineering" in machine learning, and how would you approach it for a specific problem?

Imagine you're a detective trying to solve a crime. You gather clues like fingerprints, witness testimonies, and security footage. But these clues might not be directly useful in their raw form. You need to analyse them, extract relevant information, and combine them in meaningful ways to build a strong case.

Feature engineering in machine learning is similar. It's the process of transforming raw data into features that are more informative and relevant for the AI model to learn from. It's like preparing the ingredients before cooking a delicious meal.

For example, if you're building a model to predict customer churn, you might extract features like the customer's age, purchase history, and engagement with the product or service. You might also combine these features to create new ones, like the customer's lifetime value or their recency of purchase.

The importance of feature engineering lies in its ability to improve the accuracy and efficiency of the AI model. By selecting and transforming the right features, you can help the model focus on the most relevant information and avoid being distracted by irrelevant details.

My approach to feature engineering would involve:

1. **Understanding the problem and the data:** What are the business goals? What are the characteristics of the data?
2. **Brainstorming potential features:** What information might be relevant for the AI model to learn from?
3. **Extracting and transforming features:** Use techniques like scaling, encoding, and aggregation to create new features.
4. **Selecting the most relevant features:** Use feature selection techniques to identify the most informative features.

5. **Evaluating the impact of features:** Monitor the model's performance with different sets of features.

   By carefully crafting the right features, I can help the AI model achieve its full potential and deliver valuable insights.

84
Explain the concept of "cross-validation" in machine learning to a non-technical audience, using a simple analogy.

Imagine you're a teacher trying to assess your students' understanding of a subject. You could give them one big exam at the end of the semester, but that might not be a fair assessment, as some students might have a bad day or the exam might not cover all the topics adequately.

Cross-validation in machine learning is like giving your students multiple smaller quizzes throughout the semester. You divide the class into groups, give each group a different quiz, and then combine the results to get a more comprehensive understanding of their overall knowledge.

Similarly, in cross-validation, you divide the data into multiple folds, train the AI model on different combinations of these folds, and then average the results to get a more robust estimate of the model's performance. This helps you avoid overfitting and ensures that the model can generalize well to new, unseen data.

It's like testing the AI model on different "quizzes" to make sure it has truly learned the underlying patterns in the data and not just memorized the specific examples it was trained on.

This simple analogy can help explain a complex concept like cross-validation in a way that anyone can understand, highlighting its importance in evaluating the performance of machine learning models and ensuring their reliability.

85
What is the difference between "precision" and "recall" in machine learning, and how do they relate to the "F1-score"?

Imagine you're a detective trying to catch a group of criminals. You set up a trap and catch a few suspects. Now, you need to determine how successful your operation was.

- **Precision** is like asking: "Of all the people we caught, how many were actually criminals?" It measures the accuracy of your positive predictions. A high precision means you caught mostly criminals and didn't waste time on innocent people.
- **Recall** is like asking: "Of all the actual criminals out there, how many did we manage to catch?" It measures the completeness of your predictions. A high recall means you caught most of the criminals and didn't miss many.

Ideally, you want both high precision and high recall, meaning you caught most of the criminals without wrongly accusing innocent people. However, there's often a trade-off between the two.

The **F1-score** is a way to combine precision and recall into a single metric that balances both aspects. It's like calculating the average of your precision and recall scores. A high F1-score indicates a good balance between catching criminals and avoiding false alarms.

These metrics are important for evaluating the performance of machine learning models, especially in tasks like fraud detection, medical diagnosis, and information retrieval, where both false positives and false negatives can have significant consequences.

86
How would you explain the concept of "hyperparameter tuning" in machine learning to a non-technical audience, using a simple analogy?

Imagine you're baking a cake. You have a recipe, but it allows for some flexibility. You can adjust the amount of sugar, the baking time, and the oven temperature to get the perfect cake.

Hyperparameter tuning in machine learning is similar. You have an AI model with some adjustable settings, called hyperparameters. These hyperparameters control the learning process and can affect the model's performance.

For example, in a decision tree model, the maximum depth of the tree is a hyperparameter. A deeper tree can capture more complex patterns, but it might also overfit the training data.

Hyperparameter tuning is like experimenting with different settings to find the optimal combination that produces the best cake (or the best AI model). You try different values for the hyperparameters, evaluate the model's performance, and adjust the settings until you get the desired results.

It's like fine-tuning the recipe to get the perfect balance of sweetness, texture, and flavour. In machine learning, this fine-tuning can significantly improve the model's accuracy and efficiency.

This simple analogy can help explain a complex concept like hyperparameter tuning in a way that anyone can understand, highlighting its importance in optimizing machine learning models and achieving the best possible results.

87
What is the difference between a "generative" and a "discriminative" machine learning model, and can you give examples of each?

Imagine you're an artist. You can either create something new, like painting a picture from scratch, or you can discriminate between existing things, like judging a painting competition.

- **Generative models** in machine learning are like the creative artists. They learn the underlying patterns and structure of the data and then generate new examples that resemble the training data. Think of them as "inventors" of new data.
  - **Example:** A generative model can create realistic images of faces, compose new music, or write different styles of text.

- **Discriminative models** are like the art judges. They learn to distinguish between different categories or classes of data. Think of them as "classifiers" or "predictors."
  - **Example:** A discriminative model can classify emails as spam or not spam, predict customer churn, or diagnose diseases.

The key difference is that generative models focus on creating new data, while discriminative models focus on classifying or predicting existing data.

Here's a table (on next page) summarizing the key differences:

Feature	Generative Models	Discriminative Models
Goal	Generate new data	Classify or predict existing data
Focus	Underlying data distribution	Decision boundary between classes
Examples	Image generation, text generation, music composition	Image classification, spam filtering, fraud detection

Understanding the difference between these two types of models can help developers choose the right approach for their specific needs and build more effective AI solutions.

88
Explain the concept of "ensemble learning" in machine learning to a non-technical audience, using a simple analogy.

Imagine you're trying to make an important decision, like choosing a new car. You wouldn't just rely on one source of information, like a single review or a friend's opinion. You'd gather information from multiple sources, like reading reviews, talking to experts, and comparing prices, to make a more informed decision.

Ensemble learning in machine learning is similar. It's like combining the predictions of multiple AI models to get a more accurate and robust result. It's like having a team of experts working together to solve a problem, each contributing their unique perspective and expertise.

For example, imagine you're building a model to predict customer churn. You could train different types of models, like decision trees, support vector machines, and neural networks, and then combine their predictions to get a more accurate prediction.

Ensemble learning can be particularly useful when dealing with complex problems or noisy data, as it can help reduce the impact of individual model errors and improve overall performance. It's like having a diverse team of experts, where the strengths of one expert can compensate for the weaknesses of another.

This simple analogy can help explain a complex concept like ensemble learning in a way that anyone can understand, highlighting its potential to improve the accuracy and reliability of machine learning models.

89
What is the difference between "bagging" and "boosting" in ensemble learning, and can you give examples of algorithms that use each technique?

Imagine you're trying to predict the winner of a horse race. You can use two different strategies to combine the opinions of multiple experts:

- **Bagging** is like asking each expert to make their prediction independently, without knowing what the others are saying. You then combine their predictions by taking a majority vote or averaging their probabilities. This helps reduce the impact of individual biases and errors.
  - **Example:** Random Forest is a popular bagging algorithm that combines multiple decision trees.

- **Boosting** is like asking the experts to make their predictions sequentially, with each expert focusing on the mistakes made by the previous ones. This helps improve the overall accuracy by focusing on the difficult cases.

  - **Example:** AdaBoost and Gradient Boosting are popular boosting algorithms that iteratively improve the model's performance.

The key difference is that bagging combines independent predictions, while boosting combines sequential predictions that learn from previous mistakes.

Here's a table (on next page) summarizing the key differences:

Feature	Bagging	Boosting
Combina tion	Independent predictions	Sequential predictions
Focus	Reducing variance and overfitting	Improving accuracy and reducing bias
Examples	Random Forest	AdaBoost, Gradient Boosting

Understanding the difference between these two ensembles learning techniques can help developers choose the right approach for their specific needs and build more effective AI models.

90
How would you explain the concept of "dimensionality reduction" in machine learning to a non-technical audience, using a simple analogy?

Imagine you're trying to organize a messy closet. You have clothes, shoes, accessories, and other items piled up everywhere. To make it more organized, you could group similar items together, like putting all the shirts in one drawer, all the pants in another, and all the shoes on a shelf.

Dimensionality reduction in machine learning is similar. It's like organizing the data by grouping similar features together, reducing the number of variables while preserving the essential information.

For example, imagine you have a dataset with hundreds of features about customers, like their age, income, purchase history, and social media activity. Dimensionality reduction techniques can help you identify the most important features that capture the essence of the data, reducing the complexity and making it easier to analyse and visualize.

It's like decluttering the closet and keeping only the essential items, making it more manageable and efficient. In machine learning, this can improve the performance of the AI model by reducing noise and redundancy in the data.

This simple analogy can help explain a complex concept like dimensionality reduction in a way that anyone can understand, highlighting its potential to simplify data analysis and improve the efficiency of machine learning models.

91
What are some ethical considerations when developing and deploying AI systems, and how would you address them as a developer?

Developing and deploying AI systems comes with great responsibility. It's crucial to consider the ethical implications and ensure that these systems are used for good and don't perpetuate harmful biases or discriminate against certain groups. Here are some key ethical considerations and how I would address them as a developer:

1. Fairness and Bias:

- **Challenge:** AI systems can inherit and amplify biases present in the data they are trained on, leading to unfair or discriminatory outcomes.
- **Solution:** Use diverse and representative datasets, carefully evaluate model performance across different demographics, and employ techniques like fairness-aware learning to mitigate bias.

2. Privacy and Security:

- **Challenge:** AI systems often process sensitive personal data, raising concerns about privacy violations and data breaches.
- **Solution:** Implement strong data protection measures, ensure compliance with privacy regulations, and prioritize data anonymization and encryption whenever possible.

3. Transparency and Explainability:

- **Challenge:** Complex AI systems can be difficult to understand, making it challenging to explain their decisions and build trust with users.
- **Solution:** Use interpretable models or techniques like SHAP values to explain predictions. Be transparent about the limitations of the AI system and provide clear information to users about how their data is being used.

4. Accountability and Responsibility:

- **Challenge:** Determining who is responsible for the decisions made by an AI system can be complex, especially in autonomous systems.
- **Solution:** Establish clear lines of responsibility and accountability for AI systems. Develop mechanisms for human oversight and intervention when necessary.

5. Societal Impact:

- **Challenge:** AI systems can have far-reaching societal impacts, including job displacement and the potential for misuse.
- **Solution:** Consider the potential societal impact of AI systems and engage in discussions with stakeholders to address concerns and ensure responsible development and deployment.

As a developer, I would prioritize ethical considerations throughout the AI development lifecycle, from data collection and model training to deployment and monitoring. I would strive to build AI systems that are fair, transparent, secure, and beneficial to society.

92
What are some key differences between traditional machine learning models and generative AI models?

While both traditional machine learning and generative AI models learn from data, they have distinct goals and approaches:

- **Traditional machine learning** models typically focus on **predicting or classifying** existing data. They learn patterns and relationships in the data to make predictions about unseen data, like predicting customer churn or classifying images.

- **Generative AI** models, on the other hand, focus on **creating new data** that resembles the training data. They learn the underlying distribution of the data and then generate new samples from that distribution, like creating realistic images or composing music.

Here's a table summarizing the key differences:

Feature	Traditional Machine Learning	Generative AI
Goal	Predict or classify existing data	Generate new data
Focus	Patterns and relationships in data	Underlying data distribution
Examples	Classification, regression, clustering	Image generation, text generation, music composition

93
What are some popular architectures used in generative AI models, and what are their strengths and weaknesses?

Several popular architectures are used in generative AI models, each with its own strengths and weaknesses:

1. Generative Adversarial Networks (GANs):

- **Concept:** GANs consist of two neural networks, a generator and a discriminator, that compete against each other. The generator creates new data samples, while the discriminator tries to distinguish between real and generated samples. This adversarial process pushes both networks to improve, leading to more realistic and convincing generated data.
- **Strengths:** Can generate high-quality, realistic data samples.
- **Weaknesses:** Can be difficult to train and stabilize. Prone to mode collapse, where the generator produces limited variations of the data.

2. Variational Autoencoders (VAEs):

- **Concept:** VAEs learn a compressed representation of the data and then use this representation to generate new samples. They are based on the idea of encoding the data into a lower-dimensional latent space and then decoding it back to the original space.
- **Strengths:** Can learn smooth and continuous representations of the data. Can generate diverse samples.
- **Weaknesses:** Generated samples can be blurry or less sharp compared to GANs.

3. Autoregressive Models:

- **Concept:** Autoregressive models generate data sequentially, predicting the next element based on the previous ones. They are commonly used for text and music generation.
- **Strengths:** Can generate coherent and structured sequences.
- **Weaknesses:** Can be slow to generate long sequences. Prone to repetition and lack of long-term dependencies.

4. Diffusion Models:

- **Concept:** Diffusion models gradually add noise to the data until it becomes pure noise, and then learn to reverse this process to generate new data from noise.
- **Strengths:** Can generate high-quality and diverse samples. Can handle complex data distributions.
- **Weaknesses:** Can be computationally expensive to train and sample from.

Choosing the right architecture depends on the specific task and the desired characteristics of the generated data. GANs are often preferred for generating realistic images, while VAEs are suitable for learning smooth representations and generating diverse samples. Autoregressive models are commonly used for text and music generation, and diffusion models are gaining popularity for their ability to generate high-quality samples from complex data distributions.

94
What are some common challenges in training generative AI models, and how can they be addressed?

Training generative AI models can be challenging due to various factors, including data requirements, computational resources, and the need to balance creativity and control. Here are some common challenges and potential solutions:

1. Data Requirements:

- **Challenge:** Generative models often require large and diverse datasets to learn the underlying data distribution effectively. Obtaining such datasets can be difficult and expensive.
- **Solution:** Use data augmentation techniques to increase the size and diversity of the training data. Explore synthetic data generation or transfer learning from pre-trained models to overcome data limitations.

2. Computational Resources:

- **Challenge:** Training large generative models can be computationally expensive, requiring powerful hardware and significant time.
- **Solution:** Utilize cloud-based platforms with GPUs or TPUs to accelerate training. Optimize model architectures and training algorithms for efficiency. Explore distributed training techniques to leverage multiple machines.

3. Mode Collapse:

- **Challenge:** GANs are prone to mode collapse, where the generator produces limited variations of the data, failing to capture the full diversity of the training set.
- **Solution:** Use techniques like minibatch discrimination or feature matching to encourage the generator to explore different modes of the data distribution.

4. Evaluation Metrics:

- **Challenge:** Evaluating the quality and diversity of generated data can be subjective and challenging. Traditional metrics like accuracy or precision may not be suitable for generative models.
- **Solution:** Use a combination of quantitative and qualitative evaluation metrics. Explore metrics like Inception Score (IS) or Fréchet Inception Distance (FID) to assess the quality and diversity of generated images. Utilize human evaluation for subjective assessment.

5. Control and Stability:

- **Challenge:** Controlling the output of generative models and ensuring stability during training can be difficult.
- **Solution:** Use techniques like conditional generation to guide the generation process. Explore different loss functions and regularization techniques to improve stability.

By addressing these challenges, developers can train more effective and reliable generative AI models, unlocking their potential for creative applications and innovation.

95
What are some potential applications of generative AI in various industries, such as healthcare, finance, and entertainment?

Generative AI is poised to revolutionize various industries by enabling the creation of new content, automating tasks, and providing personalized experiences. Here are some potential applications:

Healthcare:

- **Drug discovery:** Generate new drug candidates and predict their efficacy.
- **Medical imaging:** Generate synthetic medical images for training and research.
- **Personalized medicine:** Create personalized treatment plans based on patient data.
- **Prosthetics design:** Generate customized prosthetic designs based on individual needs.

Finance:

- **Fraud detection:** Generate synthetic fraud data to train detection models.
- **Algorithmic trading:** Generate trading strategies and optimize investment portfolios.
- **Risk management:** Generate scenarios to assess and mitigate financial risks.
- **Personalized financial advice:** Create customized financial plans and investment recommendations.

Entertainment:

- **Content creation:** Generate music, scripts, and video game levels.
- **Personalized recommendations:** Create personalized entertainment recommendations based on user preferences.
- **Interactive experiences:** Generate interactive narratives and virtual worlds.
- **Special effects and animation:** Generate realistic special effects and animations for movies and games.

Other Industries:

- **Manufacturing:** Generate designs for new products and optimize production processes.
- **Education:** Generate personalized learning materials and assessments.
- **Marketing:** Generate personalized advertising campaigns and product recommendations.
- **Fashion:** Generate new clothing designs and personalize fashion recommendations.

These are just a few examples of the many potential applications of generative AI. As the technology continues to evolve, we can expect to see even more innovative and impactful uses across various industries.

96
What are some of the ethical concerns surrounding the use of generative AI, and how can they be addressed?

Generative AI, while offering tremendous potential, also raises ethical concerns that need careful consideration and proactive solutions. Here are some key concerns:

1. Misinformation and Manipulation:

- **Challenge:** Generative AI can be used to create convincing fake content, such as deepfakes or synthetic text, which can be used to spread misinformation, manipulate public opinion, or damage reputations.
- **Solution:** Develop detection tools and techniques to identify generated content. Promote media literacy and critical thinking skills. Establish ethical guidelines and regulations for the responsible use of generative AI.

2. Bias and Discrimination:

- **Challenge:** Generative models can inherit and amplify biases present in the training data, leading to discriminatory or unfair outcomes, such as generating stereotypical images or biased text.
- **Solution:** Use diverse and representative datasets. Employ fairness-aware learning techniques to mitigate bias. Conduct regular audits and evaluations to identify and address potential biases in generated content.

3. Job Displacement:

- **Challenge:** Generative AI can automate tasks previously performed by humans, potentially leading to job displacement in creative industries like writing, art, and music.
- **Solution:** Invest in education and training programs to help workers adapt to new roles and skills. Explore new economic models and social safety nets to support those affected by automation.

4. Intellectual Property:

- **Challenge:** Generative AI raises questions about ownership and copyright of generated content. Who owns the rights to a song composed by an AI or an image created by a GAN?
- **Solution:** Develop clear legal frameworks and guidelines for intellectual property rights in the context of generative AI. Explore new models of ownership and collaboration between humans and AI.

5. Environmental Impact:

- **Challenge:** Training large generative models can require significant computational resources, leading to increased energy consumption and carbon emissions.
- **Solution:** Develop more energy-efficient training algorithms and hardware. Explore the use of renewable energy sources for AI development and deployment.

Addressing these ethical concerns requires a multi-faceted approach involving collaboration between researchers, developers, policymakers, and the public. By promoting responsible development and deployment of generative AI, we can harness its potential for good while mitigating its risks.

97
How can generative AI be used to improve education and learning experiences?

Generative AI has the potential to revolutionize education by creating personalized learning experiences, generating engaging content, and providing individualized support to students. Here are some ways it can be used:

- **Personalized Learning:** Generative AI can create customized learning paths and materials based on individual student needs and preferences. It can analyse student performance, identify learning gaps, and generate targeted exercises and resources to address those gaps.
- **Interactive Content:** Generative AI can create interactive simulations, games, and virtual environments that make learning more engaging and immersive. It can generate realistic scenarios and challenges that help students apply their knowledge and develop critical thinking skills.
- **Automated Feedback and Assessment:** Generative AI can provide automated feedback on student work, identifying errors and suggesting improvements. It can also generate personalized assessments that adapt to student progress and provide a more accurate measure of their understanding.
- **Assistive Technologies:** Generative AI can power assistive technologies for students with disabilities, such as text-to-speech and speech-to-text tools, personalized learning interfaces, and adaptive learning platforms.
- **Teacher Support:** Generative AI can assist teachers by automating administrative tasks, generating lesson plans, and providing insights into student performance. This can free up teachers to focus on individualized instruction and student interaction.

By leveraging the power of generative AI, we can create more personalized, engaging, and effective learning experiences for all students, regardless of their background or learning style.

98
How can generative AI be used to accelerate scientific discovery and innovation?

Generative AI is poised to become a powerful tool for scientists and researchers, helping them analyse data, generate hypotheses, and design experiments more efficiently. Here are some ways it can accelerate scientific discovery and innovation:

- **Data Analysis and Pattern Recognition:** Generative AI can analyse vast amounts of scientific data, identify patterns and anomalies, and generate insights that might be missed by traditional methods. This can lead to new discoveries and a deeper understanding of complex phenomena.
- **Hypothesis Generation:** Generative AI can generate new hypotheses and research directions by exploring different combinations of variables and parameters. This can help scientists identify promising areas for further investigation and accelerate the pace of discovery.
- **Experiment Design and Optimization:** Generative AI can help design and optimize experiments by simulating different scenarios and predicting outcomes. This can reduce the time and resources required for experimentation and lead to more efficient research.
- **Drug Discovery and Development:** Generative AI can be used to generate new drug candidates, predict their efficacy and safety, and even design personalized therapies tailored to individual patients. This can accelerate the drug development process and lead to more effective treatments.
- **Materials Science:** Generative AI can be used to design new materials with specific properties, such as strength, conductivity, or heat resistance. This can lead to the development of new materials for various applications, from electronics to construction.

By leveraging the power of generative AI, scientists can accelerate the pace of discovery, make more informed decisions, and push the boundaries of human knowledge.

99

If you could use generative AI to create any tool or application to solve a real-world problem, what would it be and why?

If I could harness the power of generative AI to create a tool, I would build an **"AI-Powered Personalized Education Platform."** This platform would revolutionize education by providing customized learning experiences tailored to each student's unique needs, strengths, and learning styles.

Here's how it would work:

- **Personalized Learning Paths:** The platform would analyse a student's performance, identify knowledge gaps, and generate customized learning paths with relevant resources, exercises, and challenges.
- **Adaptive Content Generation:** It would create interactive simulations, games, and virtual environments that adapt to the student's progress and provide engaging learning experiences.
- **AI Tutoring and Feedback:** The platform would offer AI-powered tutoring and personalized feedback on student work, helping them understand concepts, correct mistakes, and improve their skills.
- **Multilingual Support:** It would provide support in multiple languages, making education accessible to students from diverse backgrounds.
- **Accessibility Features:** The platform would incorporate accessibility features for students with disabilities, such as text-to-speech, speech-to-text, and personalized learning interfaces.

This AI-powered education platform would democratize education, making it more accessible, engaging, and effective for everyone. It would empower students to learn at their own pace, in their own way, and reach their full potential.

Why this tool?

Education is the foundation for individual growth and societal progress. Yet, traditional education systems often struggle to cater to the diverse needs of students. This AI-powered platform would address this challenge by providing personalized learning experiences that empower every student to succeed. It would break down barriers to education, promote lifelong learning, and contribute to a more equitable and informed society.

100
Some people fear that generative AI will eventually replace human creativity and jobs. How would you respond to these concerns, and what opportunities do you see for humans and AI to collaborate in the future?

It's understandable that some people fear generative AI will replace human creativity and jobs. After all, AI can now generate text, images, music, and even code, tasks that were once considered uniquely human. However, I believe this fear is misplaced.

Generative AI is a tool, not a replacement for human creativity. It can automate tasks, generate ideas, and even create impressive content, but it lacks the spark of true creativity, the ability to connect with human emotions, and the understanding of context and nuance that humans possess.

Instead of replacing human creativity, generative AI can **augment and enhance it.** Imagine writers using AI to overcome writer's block, artists using AI to explore new styles and mediums, and musicians using AI to compose complex harmonies and melodies. AI can be a powerful tool for collaboration, pushing the boundaries of human creativity and unlocking new possibilities.

As for jobs, while some jobs may be automated by AI, **new jobs and opportunities will also emerge.** We will need people to design, develop, train, and maintain AI systems, as well as people who can interpret and apply the insights generated by AI. Moreover, AI can free humans from tedious and repetitive tasks, allowing them to focus on more creative and fulfilling work.

The key is to embrace AI as a partner, not a competitor. By collaborating with AI, we can leverage its strengths while retaining our uniquely human qualities. This collaboration can lead to new forms of art, new scientific discoveries, and new solutions to complex problems.

Opportunities for collaboration:

- **Human-AI co-creation:** Artists and AI working together to create new forms of art and expression.
- **AI-assisted problem-solving:** Scientists and researchers using AI to analyse data, generate hypotheses, and design experiments.
- **Personalized education:** AI tutors and personalized learning platforms helping students learn more effectively.
- **Accessible healthcare:** AI-powered diagnostic tools and personalized treatment plans improving patient outcomes.

By embracing collaboration and focusing on the unique strengths of both humans and AI, we can create a future where AI enhances our lives and empowers us to achieve more than ever before.

101

Imagine a world where generative AI is widely accessible to everyone. What are some potential benefits and risks of this democratization of AI, and how can we ensure that it is used responsibly and ethically?

A world where generative AI is widely accessible to everyone holds both immense promise and potential peril. Let's explore the potential benefits and risks, along with strategies to ensure responsible and ethical use:

Potential Benefits:

- **Increased Creativity and Innovation:** Democratizing generative AI can unleash a wave of creativity and innovation, empowering individuals, businesses, and communities to generate new ideas, products, and solutions. Imagine artists, writers, musicians, and entrepreneurs using AI tools to express themselves, create new forms of art, and build innovative businesses.
- **Improved Productivity and Efficiency:** Generative AI can automate tasks, analyse data, and generate insights, leading to increased productivity and efficiency across various industries. This can free up human workers to focus on more creative, strategic, and fulfilling tasks.
- **Enhanced Accessibility and Inclusion:** Generative AI can create personalized experiences, adaptive technologies, and assistive tools that cater to diverse needs and abilities. This can make technology more accessible and inclusive for everyone, regardless of their background or circumstances.
- **Accelerated Scientific Discovery:** Generative AI can accelerate scientific discovery and innovation by analysing data, generating hypotheses, and designing experiments more efficiently. This can lead to breakthroughs in medicine, materials science, environmental science, and other fields.
- **Enhanced Education and Learning:** Generative AI can create personalized learning experiences, interactive content, and adaptive assessments, making education more engaging and effective for all students.

Potential Risks:

- **Misinformation and Manipulation:** The widespread availability of generative AI can increase the risk of misinformation and manipulation, as malicious actors can use AI to create convincing fake content and spread propaganda.
- **Bias and Discrimination:** If not developed and deployed responsibly, generative AI can perpetuate and amplify existing biases, leading to discriminatory outcomes and unfair treatment of certain groups.
- **Job Displacement and Economic Inequality:** The automation potential of generative AI can lead to job displacement and exacerbate economic inequality if not managed carefully.
- **Privacy and Security Concerns:** The widespread use of generative AI can raise concerns about privacy violations and data breaches, especially if sensitive personal data is used to train or operate AI systems.
- **Erosion of Trust and Authenticity:** The ability to generate realistic fake content can erode trust in information and institutions, making it difficult to distinguish between authentic and fabricated content.

Ensuring Responsible and Ethical Use:

- **Develop Ethical Guidelines and Regulations:** Establish clear ethical guidelines and regulations for the development and deployment of generative AI, focusing on fairness, transparency, accountability, and privacy.
- **Promote Education and Awareness:** Educate the public about the potential benefits and risks of generative AI, promote media literacy and critical thinking skills, and encourage responsible use of AI tools.
- **Invest in Research and Development:** Invest in research and development of AI safety and security measures, such as detection tools for generated content, fairness-aware learning algorithms, and privacy-preserving technologies.
- **Foster Collaboration and Dialogue:** Foster collaboration and dialogue between researchers, developers, policymakers, and the public to address ethical concerns and ensure that generative AI is used for good.
- **Empower Individuals and Communities:** Empower individuals and communities to use generative AI responsibly and ethically, providing them with the tools and knowledge they need to make informed decisions and contribute to a positive future for AI.

By addressing these challenges and promoting responsible use, we can harness the transformative power of generative AI to create a more creative, inclusive, and innovative future for everyone.

"Thank you for reading.
Your support means
the world to me."